Tomato Bisque for the BRAIN

A Book of Psychological Wisdom and Empowerment, Inspirational Quotes, and Positive Affirmations

David A. Wright, MD, MM, MBA, MHSA (Dr. David)

Tomato Bisque for the Brain

A Book of Psychological Wisdom and Empowerment,
Inspirational Quotes, and Positive Affirmations

David A. Wright, MD, MM, MBA, MHSA (Dr. David)

TOMATO BISQUE FOR THE BRAIN
A BOOK OF PSYCHOLOGICAL WISDOM AND EMPOWERMENT,
INSPIRATIONAL QUOTES, AND POSITIVE AFFIRMATIONS

iUniverse books may be ordered through booksellers or by contacting:

iUniverse
1663 Liberty Drive
Bloomington, IN 47403
www.iuniverse.com
844-349-9409

ISBN: 978-1-6632-0989-4 (sc)
ISBN: 978-1-6632-0988-7 (e)

Library of Congress Control Number: 2021904348

Print information available on the last page.

iUniverse rev. date: 04/30/2021

Use *Tomato Bisque for the Brain* to help empower your ambitions.

Use *Tomato Bisque for the Brain* to help inspire your desire for success.

Use *Tomato Bisque for the Brain* to help fuel your daily meditations.

Use *Tomato Bisque for the Brain* to help fuel your dreams and aspirations.

Use *Tomato Bisque for the Brain* to help fuel your hypnosis sessions.

Use *Tomato Bisque for the Brain* to help energize your mind, body, spirit, soul, and psyche.

Use *Tomato Bisque for the Brain* to help you stay mentally refreshed and renewed.

Use *Tomato Bisque for the Brain* in your thoughts and prayers.

Turn the quotations in chapter 7 into positive self-affirmations.

Turn the statements and phrases in chapter 7 into I-statements and self-affirmations.

Tomato Bisque for the Brain is nourishment for your mind, body, spirit, soul, and psyche.

Tear out your favorite pages and post them in prominent places where you will see them on a regular basis.

Add the phrases, quotations, and affirmations herein to your daily living, habits and practices.

Similar to my suggestions for my first book, *Sweet Potato Pie for the Spirit, Soul, and Psyche*, if you have little to no interest in emotional conditioning (chapter 1), creating a support network for success (chapter 2), how to quickly and easily reset your mindset after a bad experience, a tough day, or a challenging obstacle (chapter 3), how to use sound and music to change your mood (chapter 4), how to use mental images and pictures to create the life that you desire (chapter 5), or how to stay focused, centered, balanced, and productive when life gets hectic (chapter 6), then by all means feel free to go straight to the soup (chapter 7).

SELF IMPROVEMENT

Tomato Bisque for the Brain is a book of wisdom, abundance, empowerment, prosperity and success.
- It is the best way to increase your self-improvement, self-development, self-motivation, self-reflection, self-actualization, self-determination, self-transformation and self-enhancement on a daily basis!
- In addition to carrying 2/3rds of a year's worth of motivational quotations and inspirational self-affirmations (in Chapter 7), this book also helps to enable you to move forward in positive, transformational ways by presenting you with techniques, methods and strategies for helping you control your mood, create success, sideswipe negativity, escape emotional and behavioral ruts, and reset your mindset when needed.

- Chapter One covers Emotion Hoarding
- Chapter Two covers how to create circles of trust, empowerment and abundance in your life
- Chapter Three shows you how to create and press the "RESET" Switch in life
- Chapter Four covers the power of sound and music to enhance life
- Chapter Five covers the topic of mental imagery to create the future that you desire
- Chapter Six contains a sure psychological strategy for prioritizing tasks and simplifying the process of decision-making
- Chapter Seven provides you with two thirds (2/3) of a year of motivational quotes, inspirational phrases and daily positive self-affirmations

Together, the chapters of this book will empower you with success-driving techniques while also providing you with the basic concepts, underpinnings and foundation for the formation of the habits upon which healthy mindsets and success are built.

—David A. Wright, MD, MM, MBA, MHSA

"Tomato Bisque for the Brain is inspiring. It taps into the very essence of self-esteem building and affirmation. Dr. Wright manages to boost the spirits of readers by employing short, straight-to-the-point quotes that are enabling, timely, emotionally tranquilizing, and useful for readers. These quotes are spiritually rich in nature and can, like a hot bowl of tomato bisque soup, indeed lift your spirits, allay your cravings, and comfort you."

—Dr. Bettye Dunn-Wright
University of Arkansas at Pine Bluff
Associate Professor, School of Education, Curriculum and Instruction
Past School District Superintendent & Elementary School Principal

"Tomato Bisque for the Brain is an outstanding addition to the motivational self-help field as we have been awaiting a compendium of practical self-help quotes and positive affirmations. Individuals struggling with stress, anxiety, life direction, or challenges and obstacles will find this immensely valuable. I have known Dr. Wright for over ten years. He is an intelligent, observant, levelheaded, practical, and innovative thinker in the mental health field. This should be required reading for all individuals who struggle with purpose and direction!"

—Todd M. Antin, MD
Board certified in adult, addiction, forensic, and geriatric psychiatry
CEO and Medical Director of PACT Atlanta LLC
Psychiatry Department Medical Director for Emory DeKalb Medical Center

U.S. $XX.XX
ISBN 978-1-6632-0989-4

www.iuniverse.com

Tomato Bisque for the BRAIN

A Book of Psychological Wisdom and Empowerment,
Inspirational Quotes, and Positive Affirmations

David A. Wright, MD, MM, MBA, MHSA (Dr. David)

CONTENTS

FOREWORD

Tomato Bisque for the Brain is inspiring, and it taps into the very essence of self-esteem building and affirmation. Dr. Wright manages to boost the spirit of readers within Chapter 7 by employing short, straight-to-the-point quotes that are enabling, timely, emotionally tranquilizing, and useful for readers. These quotes are categorized, accessible, and ready to lift the spirits of readers as desired or needed. Many of the quotes are spiritually rich in nature and can, like a hot bowl of tomato bisque soup, indeed, lift your spirit, allay your cravings, and comfort you.

Dr. Bettye Dunn-Wright

University of Arkansas at Pine Bluff (UAPB)

Associate Professor, School of Education, Curriculum, and Instruction

Past School Superintendent, Principal, and Teacher

FOREWORD

Tomato Bisque for the Brain is an outstanding addition to the motivational self-help field as we have been awaiting a compendium of practical self-help quotes and positive affirmations. Clients struggling with depression, low self-esteem, or poor social support will find this immensely valuable. I have known Dr. Wright for over ten years. He is an intelligent, observant, levelheaded, practical, and innovative thinker in the mental health field. This should be required reading for all individuals who struggle with purpose and direction!

Todd M. Antin, MD
Board certified in adult, addiction, forensic, and geriatric psychiatry
CEO and medical director of PACT Atlanta LLC

INTRODUCTION

The idea for *Tomato Bisque for the Brain* came from watching episodes of *Super Soul Sunday* on the Oprah Winfrey Network (OWN). Watching the show has been such an inspiration to me. It's been a true teacher. Oprah's *Thought for Today* newsletter has also been a great inspiration. As an MD with an abundance, empowerment, mind-setting, and prosperity practice, I help my clients to realize that there are motivations, inspirations, and moments of insight that are readily available to them on a daily basis. I found myself continually sending them to other sources to find concepts, affirmations, quotes, and statements that would help empower them and fuel their meditations. Eventually, I decided to create such a source for them so that I wouldn't have to necessarily send them elsewhere.

I believe that we should find and share positive energy when and where we can. *Tomato Bisque for the Brain* represents my opportunity to share the positive energy and encouragement that I've received from my parents, Reverend Harlis R. Wright and Dr. Bettye D. Wright; my mentor, Dr. Todd M. Antin; Dr. Oprah Winfrey; my teachers Mrs. Ollie Baron (second grade), Mrs. Dorothy Holt (high school French), Mrs. Rose Jones (third grade), Mayor Shirley Washington (fourth grade), Mr. Nathaniel Grant (fifth grade), Mrs. Hales (sixth grade), Mrs. Clowers (sixth grade), Mrs. Vonna Woods (fifth grade), Mr. Marty Seewald (high school acapella choir), and Coach Bill Cleveland (intermediate school—seventh grade); my friends; my coworkers; life circumstances; and other sources. I hope that the concepts, affirmations, quotes, and phrases in *Tomato Bisque for the Brain* inspire you as much as others have inspired me.

In addition to carrying two-thirds of a year's worth of motivational quotations and inspirational self-affirmations (in chapter 7), *Tomato Bisque for the Brain* also helps to enable you to move forward in positive, transformational ways by presenting you with techniques, methods, and strategies for helping you control your mood, create success, sideswipe negativity, escape emotional and behavioral ruts, and reset your mindset when needed. Chapter 1 covers emotion hoarding; chapter 2 covers how to create circles of trust, empowerment, and abundance in your life; chapter 3 shows you how to create and press the reset switch in life; chapter 4 covers the power of sound and music to enhance life; chapter 5 covers the topic of mental imagery to create the future that you desire; chapter

6 contains a sure psychological strategy for prioritizing tasks and simplifying the process of decision-making; and finally, chapter 7 provides you with two-thirds of a year's worth of motivational quotes, inspirational phrases, and daily positive self-affirmations. Together, the chapters of *Tomato Bisque for the Brain* will empower you with success-driving techniques while also providing you with the basic concepts, the underpinnings, and the foundation for the formation of the habits upon which healthy mindsets are built.

Once you have begun to let go of emotional, psychological, and mental baggage, as discussed in chapter 1, you can begin surrounding yourself with like-minded individuals, coaches, mentors, and associates using the strategies in chapter 2. I like to call these "circles of trust and influence."

After you have begun to create your new associations and relationships using the concepts presented in chapter 2, you hit the reset switch by using the methods and techniques provided in chapter 3 to create a new direction and new pathways for taking empowered journeys.

Once you have hit the reset switch by using the methods and techniques provided in chapter 3 to create a new direction and new pathways for empowered journeys, you will begin to use music and sound to create a new normal (as presented within chapter 4) for your mood and your ability to focus, concentrate, and achieve your goals.

After you have begun to use music and sound to create a new normal for your mood and your ability to focus, concentrate, and achieve your goals (as presented within chapter 4), you will begin to use the power of your greatest somatic (i.e., bodily) sense and its associated mind and brain connections to start to really craft the life that you desire (as presented within chapter 5).

Once you have begun to use the power of your greatest somatic sense and its associated mind and brain connections to start to really craft the life that you desire (as presented within chapter 5), you will move on to the next chapter and start using a method that will allow you to permanently defeat procrastination so you may begin being more productive, efficient, and goal-directed than you've ever been before—using a simple system called the rank order system (ROS, as presented within chapter 6).

Finally, after you have started using the rank order system to permanently defeat procrastination and to begin being more productive, efficient, and goal-directed than you've ever been before (as presented within chapter 6), you will begin to use the positive motivational quotations and inspiring, mindset-based, inspirational self-affirmations in chapter 7 to begin permanently changing your thoughts, feelings, and belief systems.

Together, these tools, methods, resources, strategies, and approaches will positively change the trajectory of your life—while simultaneously adding joy, happiness, and fulfillment to it! Are you ready to become *tougher*? Are you ready to become *stronger*? Are you ready to become a *fighter*? Then let's get started!

CHAPTER 1

ARE YOU AN EMOTION(AL) HOARDER?

Most people don't consider themselves to be hoarders.

Most of us don't have hordes of household items, clothing, shoes, needless objects, unlikely heirlooms, supposed antiques, or collections of junk and trash that interfere with our lives to the point that they don't allow us to have guests over and/or live productive lives in our homes.

Right?

I mean, the hoarders are those people who are on reality TV shows who hoard so much stuff that their relatives have them committed, have them put out of the house, or see then the subjects of a life intervention. Even then, many of them don't notice, realize, witness, or accept that they have a clinical problem and require professional help. These are the people who have acquired (and refuse to part with) so much stuff that they have literally sealed themselves off from parts of their homes given the extreme degree of clutter, disorganization, and chaos.

Most of us aren't like *those* people, are we?

Or are we?

Here's a thought: Very few of us are hoarders of things to that extent, but almost all of us are hoarders of negative thoughts, emotions, and energy! That's right: even you!

Here's a test to see if you're an emotional and psychological hoarder. How many of the following questions do you answer "no" or "maybe" to?

❖ I am constantly progressing from one level to a higher level, reaching new heights and bounds that are planned, noticeable, measurable, and sustainable on a regular basis (monthly, quarterly, annually, etc.).

❖ I am constantly creating new goals, objectives, and projects based on my thoughts and desires, and the vast majority (70 percent or more) of these goals and projects end with my reaching the desired goal that I can measure and see within a specific time frame (within three months, within six months, within twelve months, etc.).

❖ People rarely ask me about past projects, goals, and objectives that I haven't already completed or fully accomplished.

❖ I rarely have thoughts about painful, embarrassing, sad, or unfortunate circumstances from my past.

❖ I rarely think about what could have been had I done B or C instead of A way back when.

❖ I am nearly completely content with what I have achieved thus far. There is very little that I feel I have left to contribute to this life and/or to society.

If you answered yes to the majority of these questions, then feel free to quit reading and return to your previously scheduled task(s). Or else skip to the positive affirmations and motivational quotes in chapter 7. However, if you answered no to one of more of these questions, then you most likely have hoarded feelings, thoughts, emotions, and/or energy that no longer serve your highest purpose and potential.

The real reason you keep dropping things in life is because your psychological and emotional hands and arms are full from trying to hold on to everything from your past. You can't hold on to things and also heal from them. Nor can you hold on to everything that you have held on to so far and then take on new things given that your hands are already full, right? It doesn't work that way.

You can only control many things (i.e., quantity) successfully, efficiently, and productively in a certain amount of time (i.e., duration) while still achieving a certain degree of quality. The equation must be balanced based on who you are at the present moment.

It's up to you to *choose* whether you want to hold onto the things that drag you down or to ready yourself to let go of them so that you can grab things that will move you upward and forward.

You have to make a choice: hold on or let go! You cannot do both.

Start letting go and releasing all the junk that you've been clinging to for so long. It's only holding you back. Start letting go and releasing the baggage that is preventing you from being as successful as you desire to be!

It's true: the world will not change until you do. Your individual circumstances won't change until you do. In fact, your circumstances will only change to the degree and the extent that you change. Change always begins at the source: you. If you're not willing to change, then neither will your circumstances. Become the change that you desire most.

There's no time like the present. That's why it's a gift. Become the next successful mogul! Level up! Evolve your consciousness! Potentiate your mindset! Start with your emotional, psychological, and mental baggage.

Once you have begun to let go of emotional, psychological, and mental baggage, you can begin surrounding yourself with like-minded individuals, coaches, mentors, and associates using the strategies in the next chapter. I like to call these people your "circles of trust and influence."

The first steps to letting go of a piece of baggage is to notice it, admit it, acknowledge it's presence, name it and accept it's existence. Then you release it by thinking, feeling and verbalizing its release. Meditation and Hypnosis are great methods of doing that. Journaling it and sharing it with others are also helpful for releasing it. Generally speaking, thinking, feeling and verbalizing helps to release baggage.

CHAPTER 2

CIRCLES OF TRUST

Why do you need circles of trust?

Every time I hear someone say "I made it to the top all by myself. Not a single person helped me get here! I did it all myself! Me, myself, and I!" I just laugh.

No one, and I mean no one, makes it to the top (wherever that might be), or anywhere else for that matter, by themselves. Other people and forces help you get there, regardless of whether you notice it, realize it, recognize it, or acknowledge it.

No matter where you wind up at any particular point in time, someone else played a role in your having arrived there—even if it's just the individuals who conceived and/or gave birth to you.

Whether you realize it or not, the people who are immediately around you have a greater degree of influence over your level of success than anyone else does. These people include your acquaintances, associates, coworkers, colleagues, friends, mentors, coaches, supervisors, and managers. And the degree to which you choose them and cultivate strong relationships with them determines the degree to which you achieve success.

Following are just a few of the reasons why you should create circles of trust:

1. Wisdom, which allows you to move forward in new directions without repeating the same mistakes over again.
2. Empowerment, which allows you to ask others for help, advice, and assistance without feeling unworthy of success.
3. A desire not to re-create the wheel, which allows you to borrow strategies, tools, and approaches from experts so that you don't have to reinvent systems that others have already mastered and perfected.

4. Abundance, which allows you to realize what you can achieve by seeing what others with similar goals, desires, and ambitions have achieved already.

5. Life lessons, which allow you to gain knowledge, best practices, and wisdom without risking failure, by relying upon experience.

6. Encouragement, which allows you to receive additional motivation from mentors and others during times when your strength has been challenged.

7. Motivation, which allows you to gain the strength, tenacity, and fortitude associated with feeling as if you're doing things as part of a team with a central goal.

8. Recipes for success, which allow you to create by using perspectives from others from a multitude of backgrounds and experiences.

9. Fortitude, which allows you to brave and endure circumstances that are challenging.

10. Perseverance, which allows you to stay strong when things get tougher.

11. Self-control, which allows you to manage your EQ just as well as you manage your IQ.

12. Dos and don'ts, which allow you to create a common core of concepts, principles, and rules that reliably lead to positive outcomes, results, and success.

13. Advice, which prevents you from experiencing anxiety when you aren't sure what to do next, because you already have a solution network at your disposal.

14. Tenacity, which allows you to use different thinking hats, perspectives, resources, tools, and individuals to attack novel and evolving challenges and obstacles.

15. Guidance, which facilitates the sharing of knowledge and wisdom based on a common set of experiences.

16. Mentoring, which allows you to strengthen your competencies, skills, and learning by sharing these things with those who are less experienced than you. It also paves a road for the next generation of leaders.

17. Coaching, which allows you to learn to coach others in the same way that others have coached you, providing you with a new set of leadership skills and commodities that hold value and create currency.

18. Collaboration, which allows you to get involved with, learn about, and benefit from knowledge, wisdom, and information from industries and sectors that are normally outside your field of view.

These are just eighteen reasons why you need to create a circle of trust if success is one of your desires. There are many more I didn't list.

Just know that a circle of trust can be the difference between success and failure when it comes to reaching your goals, objectives, aims, ambitions, and purposes.

Start creating your circle of trust *today*!

Once you have begun to create your new associations and relationships using the concepts presented in chapter 2, you will hit the reset switch by using the methods and techniques provided in chapter 3 to create a new direction and new pathways for an empowered journey.

CHAPTER 3

PRESS THE RESET SWITCH

How do you reset your inner compass when your ship goes off course?

Most devices, machines and "things" that measure something (or perform a function, complex or simple) require adjustment at some point. A term for this is "CALIBRATION." If you purchase a blood pressure measuring device for home use, then you'll occasionally have to have it calibrated. Calibration is a vital step in the maintenance of some measuring function.

No voyage is a straight and narrow path without rough seas, headwinds, twists, turns, curves, rocks, glaciers, and other challenges and obstacles along the way. If that weren't the case, then we would all lose the opportunity to be purposeful, resilient, evolutionary, perseverant, flexible, fortuitous, adaptable, and dynamic. It is the trials and tribulations of life that force us to grow, mature, and evolve. The very situations and circumstances that irk us the most also make us stronger and more resilient in the process.

So, what do you do when your ship seems to be veering off course despite your best efforts, intentions, and desires?

The answer: You reset [i.e., CALIBRATE]!

By the way, in general, when you feel lost, you should do one of three things (or all of them): (1) go back to the basics, (2) reset, (3) and gain additional, trusted advice and perspectives from those who have greater experience based on the principles presented within the previous chapter that you've used to create your circle of trust.

If you choose to reset first, then the question becomes how to reset. There are several ways that you can (and should) reset the variables in your life so that you may get back on course and stay on course in the future. Here are just a few starting points:

1. Are your diet and nutrient intake sufficient? (Find this out in my other book, *The Nutrient Diet*.)

a. Do you take a multivitamin each and every day?

b. Do you intake plenty of water?

c. Do you get your water from a credible source (i.e., do you drink tap, bottled, filtered, or alkalinized water)?

d. Do you consume fast food?

e. Do you prepare your own meals?

f. Does the food on your plate resemble the rainbow?

g. Does your diet include lots of fresh fish, vegetables, and/ or fruit?

2. Are you in rhythm?

a. Do you get the right *quantity* of sleep each night?

b. Do you get the right *quality* of sleep each night?

c. Are you sleepy during daytime or work hours?

d. Do you have insomnia?

e. Do you experience nightmares or bad dreams?

f. Does your mind seem to race with stressful or anxious thoughts at night?

g. Do you fall asleep on a positive note (i.e., with positive thoughts)?

h. Do you awake with abundant, empowered, positive thoughts and affirmations?

3. Are you on a frequency of abundance?

a. Do you expect things to go well or not so well?

b. Do you dread each day or look forward to each day?

c. Do you expect the best or the worst from others?

d. Do you welcome tomorrow or dread the future?

e. Are you sure and/or confident about tomorrow?

f. Do you wake up with a positive mindset each and every morning?

g. Do you use positive affirmations and mantras each morning?

4. Are you exhausted?

a. Do you wake up not rested?

b. Do you fall asleep or nap as soon as you get home from work?

c. Do you yawn at work?

d. Are you easily irritated by others?

e. Do you make the same mistakes over and over again?

f. Are you ready to give up or to change things drastically?

5. Are you centered?

a. Do you meditate daily or weekly?

b. Do you undergo hypnosis on a regular basis?

c. Do you take steps to cleanse your body, mind, spirit, and psyche?

d. Is it easy for you to admit when you're wrong or when you make a mistake?

e. Are you quick to become angry, irritated, or frustrated?

f. Do you regularly strengthen your relationships with others?

g. Do you continuously strengthen your relationship with a force greater than yourself?

h. Do you at least occasionally take breaks from TV, radio, the news, social media, and other influential external sources?

If you answered no to any of the positive questions or yes to any of the negative questions, then it's quite possible that you could use a reset!

One of the biggest factors in your ability to be successful in your endeavors is your ability to ask for help and seek assistance. You can't—and shouldn't try to—do it alone.

The degree and the speed at which you grow as a person is directly proportional to the degree of consistency with which you make an effort to seek wisdom and guidance from others when it comes to things that are outside your area of experience and/or expertise. Even if something is within your area of expertise, chances are you don't have the ability to be objective where your own thoughts, feelings, and behaviors are concerned.

Press the reset switch!

The best way to begin resetting your direction and trajectory is by going back to the basics. Start with what you consume in terms of food, content, thoughts, messages, and energy. Use my other book *The Nutrient Diet* to start changing the quantities and concentrations of the molecules, chemicals, neurotransmitters, messengers, and hormones that your body produces. Start changing what your mind consumes on a daily basis. Lessen the amount of junk that you allow your mind to be exposed to on a regular basis. Stop watching Netflix, CNN, MSNBC, and Fox News. Start limiting the amount of time you spend watching television. Stop taking in media messages that perpetuate stress responses and reactions. Stop listening to music that promotes anger, violence, sadness, depression, loss, and negativity. Stop spending time with people who bring you down instead of empowering you. Stop consuming sugary drinks and potato chips. Stop making excuses for errors and mistakes that you keep repeating. Stop spending time with toxic people. Stop expecting other people to change your circumstances for you.

Start creating daily action plans and to-do lists. Start planning for greatness. Start expanding your social circle to include people who will challenge you to grow and evolve. Start taking accountability for your diet. Start taking charge of your time. Start building professional competencies that you can use in consulting roles outside your position with your employer. Start acknowledging that there are ways in which you can improve. Start accepting that you are not where you desire to be. Start creating goals, plans, and strategies with realistic expectations and measurable action steps. Start becoming more mature. Start becoming valuable to yourself, your family, your friends, your employer, and your community. Start becoming an asset instead of a liability. Start with your foundation, and go from there.

Once you have hit the reset switch by using the methods and techniques provided in chapter 3 to create a new direction and new pathways for an empowered journey, begin to use music and sound to create a new normal for your mood and your ability to focus, concentrate, and achieve your goals.

CHAPTER 4

THE SYNERGY OF SOUND AND THE POWER OF MUSIC

Do you understand and appreciate the power of sound and music?

We're all at least partially aware of the impact that sound and music makes on our lives. In fact, sound and music make for a highly intricate part of our lives. Sounds help us to wake up in the morning (birds chirping, cows mooing, alarm clocks beeping, radios playing, etc.), they help get us through the day (with talk radio, music stations, phones, etc.), and they help us to wind down at the end of the day (with relaxing music, meditation tracks, television, ocean waves, etc.).

Hearing is one of our primary senses. Consequently, it's one of the first senses that we use (even in utero). The ability to hear is also what helps facilitate our acquisition of language, a key requirement of successful maturation within our culture.

Sound and music are heavily integrated into our culture. We use them for both reception (i.e., to receive information) and for expression (i.e., to give information). In fact, musical expression is one of the most prized forms of expression in US culture. Consequently, it's one of the highest-paying fields for those whose music is deemed to be of high value.

Great singers are among the highest-paid performers in our nation. Some such artists and groups are (or were) top earners, for example, Whitney Houston, Janet Jackson, Celine Dione, Hall & Oates, the Commodores, Madonna, Teddy Pendergrass, Karen Carpenter, the Police, U2, Depeche Mode, Duran Duran, Tupac Shakur, Kraftwerk, Alabama, Dolly Parton, Taylor Swift, Puff Daddy, Jay-Z, Lionel Richie, Rihanna, and Samantha James.

Sounds and music are also a huge part of the religious experience at many institutions, churches, and synagogues. Religious institutions use music both to express emotions and to elicit emotions from congregants. Many individuals can honestly state that they've cried more in church than in any other place.

We also use music extensively in cultural events, including festivals, celebrations, concerts, ceremonies, and other important social activities.

However, how often do you actively utilize the power of sound and/ or music to control how you feel, act, behave, and think on a daily basis? Although some people already do so, most people do not use sounds and music to control their moods, feelings, actions, behaviors, or thoughts on a daily basis. Here's a great question: If you don't already, then why don't you?

Following are just a few of the reasons why you should be actively using sound and music to improve your life experiences, to increase your level of happiness, to pull out of a bad and/or negative mood, and to increase your probability of success in your everyday endeavors (i.e., increase your intellect, memory, recall, creativity, stamina, etc.):

➢ A Stanford University School of Medicine study showed that music engages areas of the brain that are involved with paying attention, making predictions, and updating events in the memory.[1]

➢ Musicians are found to have a superior working memory compared to nonmusicians.[2]

➢ Musical experience strengthens many of the same aspects of brain function that are impaired in individuals with language and learning difficulties, such as neural timing, which, when precise, allows differentiation between speech syllables.[3]

➢ "Cross-sectional comparisons of musicians to non-musicians have established a variety of musician enhancements in auditory skills and their neural substrates, extending from enhanced perception and neural encoding of speech, most notably in suboptimal listening conditions, to more proficient auditory working memory and auditory attention."[4]

---

[1] Mitzi Baker, "Music Moves Brain to Pay Attention, Stanford Study Finds," Stanford Medicine, accessed February 24, 2015, https://plato.stanford.edu/entries/mental-imagery/.

[2] Pallesen et al., "Cognitive Control in Auditory Working Memory Is Enhanced in Musicians," *PLOS One*, June 15, 2010, https://doi.org/10.1371/journal.pone.0011120.

[3] N. Kraus and B. Chandrasekaran, "Music Training for the Development of Auditory Skills," *Nature Reviews Neuroscience* (November 2010): 599–605.

[4] Nina Kraus and Dana L. Strait, "Emergence of Biological Markers of Musicianship with School-Based Music Instruction," *Annals of the New York Academy of Sciences* (2015).

➤ Adults who received formal music instruction as children have more robust brain stem responses to sound than peers who never participated in music lessons, and the magnitude of the response correlates with how recently training ceased. These results suggest that neural changes accompanying musical training during childhood are retained in adulthood.[5]

➤ Music therapy utilizing improvisation on hand drums helped veterans modulate their "often misdirected, exaggerated, and unrecognized emotions," with the goal being generalization of these skills to everyday life. Drumming provided an opportunity for the men to express and control their feelings and helped build a sense of connectedness and group mission.[6]

➤ Researchers from Ohio State University's Wexner Medical Center looked at how different types of music and silence were processed in the brains of twenty-one people with epilepsy. Whether listening to classical music or jazz, all the participants had much higher levels of brain wave activity when listening to music, the study found. Brain wave activity

---

[5] E. Skoe, and N. Kraus, "A Little Goes a Long Way: How the Adult Brain Is Shaped by Musical Training in Childhood," *Journal of Neuroscience* (2012): 32, 34, https://doi.org/10.1523/JNEUROSCI.1949-12.2012.

[6] J. W. Burt, "Distant Thunder: Drumming with Vietnam Veterans," *Music Therapy Perspectives* 13 (1995): 110–12; quoted in Ronna Kaplan, "Music Therapy and the Military," *Huffington Post*, March 4, 2013.

in epilepsy patients tended to synchronize more with the music, especially in the temporal lobe, the researchers said.[7]

➢ A review of twenty-three studies covering almost fifteen hundred patients found that listening to music reduced heart rate, blood pressure, and anxiety in heart disease patients.[8]

➢ In research by Ferguson and Sheldon (2013), participants who listened to upbeat classical compositions by Aaron Copland, while actively trying to feel happier, felt their moods lift more than those who passively listened to the music. This suggests that engaging with music, rather than allowing it to wash over us, gives the experience extra emotional power.[9]

➢ A study by Logeswaran et al. (2009) found that a quick blast of happy music made participants perceive others' faces as happier. The same was true for a snippet of sad music. The biggest effect was seen when people looked at faces with a neutral expression. In other words, people projected the mood of the music they were listening to onto other people's faces.[10]

---

[7]   Robert Preidt, HealthDay, August 10, 2015.

[8]   Bradt and Dileo, "Music for Stress and Anxiety Reduction in Coronary Heart Disease Patients," PubMed.Gov, 2009.

[9]   Ferguson and Sheldon, "Trying to Be Happier Really Can Work: Two Experimental Studies," *Journal of Positive Psychology* (2013).

[10]   Logeswaran et al., "Cross-Modal Transfer of Emotion by Music," *Neuroscience Letters* (2009).

➢ Four out of five Americans (80 percent) believe their music education has contributed to their level of personal fulfillment.[11]

➢ Two-thirds (67 percent) of Americans say music education provides people with a disciplined approach to solving problems.[12]

➢ Two-thirds (66 percent) of Americans say that music education prepares a person to manage the tasks of his or her job more successfully.[13]

I do hope that some of these foregoing facts resonate with you.

Sounds and music have been shown to do everything from elevating mood, to improving concentration, to reducing pain, to increasing memory, to lowering blood pressure.

Invest in listening. Invest in music. Invest in sound.

Use music to adjust and/or change your moods. If you're depressed, then listen to something uplifting or something that engages the sense to overcome adversity or challenges. Classical music is good

---

[11] Regina A. Corso, "The Glee Effect? More Americans Say Music Education Prepares People for Their Careers and Problem Solving Than in 2007," July 2014, Harris Poll.

[12] Ibid.

[13] Ibid.

for such a purpose. If you're too hyped up, then listen to something down tempo. If you're having trouble focusing, then listen to classical music, or listen to something with a slower, highly repetitive beat or rhythm. This is especially helpful for those who struggle with ADHD symptoms. For instance, when I really need to focus or concentrate, I'll listen to one of the following: (1) relaxing ocean waves, (2) classical music, or (3) the music of Jens Buchert (which I classify as ambient dance, intelligent dance, or minimalist dance).

Try using music to change your mood. I guarantee you that the outcomes will be music to your ears.

Once you have begun to use music and sound to create a new normal for your mood and your ability to focus, concentrate, and achieve your goals, begin to use the power of your greatest somatic (i.e., bodily) sense and its associated mind and brain connections to start to really craft the life that you desire!

CHAPTER 5

MENTAL IMAGERY

How can you use your mental images and pictures to create the life that you desire?

In my opinion, mental imagery, visualization, and imagination can be summed up in the following way: "Conceive. Believe. Achieve." Walt Disney expressed a similar sentiment.

Authors such as Paul R. Scheele, Lisa Nichols, and Tony Robbins are advocates of this model. They are sincere believers in the idea [i.e., model] that you have to see it to believe it and/or you have to believe it in order to see it. Phrased another way, you have to see it in order to conceive it. I'm also a strong believer in this doctrine [i.e., model].

Mental imagery is used to help people do everything from increasing their academic performance and their athletic/sports performance to creating a new sense of awareness and consciousness. It has been used to help individuals relax, relieve anxiety, relieve pain, lessen muscle aches, get past challenges, overcome obstacles, create new goals, and pursue their hopes, dreams, desires, and aspirations.

Recall the phrase "I have a dream"? Why is this phrase so powerful? Have you ever asked yourself that question?

Why are dreams important? Why are pictures important? Why are images important? Why are our mental representations vital to our success?

Well, let me provide you with some sound data on the subject:

According to one source, "The retina, which contains 150 million light-sensitive rod and cone cells, is actually an outgrowth of the brain. In the brain itself, neurons devoted to visual processing number in the hundreds of millions and take up about 30 percent of the cortex, as compared with 8 percent for touch and just 3 percent for hearing."[14]

According to Image Think,

> We do know that when our eyes are open, our vision accounts for two-thirds of the electrical activity of the brain—a full 2 billion of the 3 billion firings per second—which was the finding of neuroanatomist R. S. Fixot in a paper published in 1957. ... 40% of *all* nerve fibers connected to the brain are linked to the retina. In fact, 50% of *all* neural tissue deals with vision in some way. The nerve fibers statistic is also cited by Eric Jensen in *Brain-Based Learning*. ... In that same paper from 1957 that R. S. Fixot published in the *American Journal of Ophthalmology* (summarized above), 50% of our neural tissue is directly or indirectly related to vision. More of our neurons are dedicated to vision than the other four senses combined. In fact, we may be out-evolving our sense of smell."[15]

---

[14] Denise Grady, "The Vision Thing: Mainly in the Brain," *Discover*, 1993.

[15] "Is It True or False that Vision Rules the Brain?" Image Think, November 12, 2012.

"It is often said that 2/3 (60%+) of the brain is 'involved' in vision. However possibly less than 20% of the brain is dedicated to 'visual-only' functioning. The other 40% is doing vision + touch, or vision + motor, or vision + attention, or vision + spatial navigation, or vision + meaning, etc. There is generally a smooth gradation from areas fully-specialized to one thing to areas involved in many things."[16]

According to John Medina in his book *Brain Rules*, "In the fight for more neural real estate that's going on between our olfactory cortex and the visual cortex, vision is winning."[17]

According to one author, "The eye and brain work in a partnership to interpret conflicting signals from the outside world. Ultimately, we see whatever our brains think we should."[18]

"More than 50 percent of the cortex, the surface of the brain, is devoted to processing visual information," points out Williams, the William G. Allyn Professor of Medical Optics. "Understanding how vision works may be a key to understanding how the brain as a whole works."

---

[16]   Paul King, "How Much of the Brain Is Involved with Vision? What about Hearing, Touch, Etc.?" Quora, September 28, 2013.

[17]   "Is It True or False that Vision Rules the Brain?"

[18]   Grady, "The Vision Thing."

David A. Wright, MD, MM, MBA, MHSA (Dr. David)

"When scientists back in the 1950s met to talk about artificial intelligence, they thought that teaching a computer to play chess would be very difficult, but teaching a computer to see would be easy," says David Knill, professor of brain and cognitive sciences. Why? Because chess is hard for humans. Only the rare human with lots of practice becomes a master. But seeing appears easy for us. Even a baby can see. For that matter, insects, birds, and fish can see—albeit differently than humans. Some see better, in fact. What researchers now know is that human vision is incredibly complicated. While we've developed software that can beat the pants off the best chess master and best our brightest at *Jeopardy!*, computer models have barely scratched the surface of human vision. "We mistakenly think of human vision like a camera," says Knill. "We have this metaphor of an image being cast on the retina and we tend to think of vision as capturing images and sending them to the brain, like a video camera recording to a digital tape." But human vision is more akin to speech than photography. From infancy, our brain learns how to construct a three-dimensional environment by interpreting visual sensory signals like shape, size, and occlusion, how objects that are close obstruct the view of objects farther away. Even non-visual cues, such as sounds and self-motion, help us understand how we move in space and how to move our bodies accordingly.[19]

One report assessed outcomes of hypnotherapeutic interventions for 505 children and adolescents seen by four pediatricians over a period of one year and followed from four months to two years. Presenting problems included enuresis, acute pain, chronic pain, asthma, habit disorders, obesity, encopresis, and anxiety. Using strict criteria for determination of problem resolution (e.g., all beds dry) and recognizing that some conditions were intrinsically chronic, the authors found that 51% of these children and adolescents achieved complete resolution of the presenting problem; an additional 32% achieved significant improvement, 9% showed initial or some

[19] Susan Hagen, "The Mind's Eye: How Do We Transform an Ever-Changing Jumble of Visual Stimuli into the Rich and Coherent Three-Dimensional Perception We Know as Sight?" *Rochester Review* 74, no. 4 (March–April 2012).

improvement; and 7% demonstrated no apparent change or improvement. Children as young as three years of age effectively applied self-hypnosis techniques. In general, facility in self-hypnosis increased with age.[20]

In 2013, the *Journal of Cranio-Maxillofacial Surgery* published a study in which 24 volunteers had two wisdom teeth removed. All of the patients had one tooth removed with the help of hypnosis alone, and the second tooth was removed using standard local anesthesia, without hypnosis. Here are the reported results: "Of the subjects who underwent hypnosis, only two subjects (8.3 percent) reported pain after induction of hypnosis. In the local anesthetic group, 8 subjects (33.3 percent) reported pain. The results of the study clearly showed that patients in the hypnosis group had less pain during the first few hours post-operatively.[21]

---

[20] D. P. Kohen, K. N. Olness, S. O. Colwell, and A. Heimel, "The Use of Relaxation-Mental Imagery (Self-Hypnosis) in the Management of 505 Pediatric Behavioral Encounters," *Journal of Developmental and Behavioral Pediatrics* 5, no. 1 (February 1984): 21–25.

[21] Vance Romane, "Hypnotic Pain Control, and the Power of Affirmations versus Mental Imagery," March 10, 2016, VanceRomane.com.

Mental imagery is a familiar aspect of most people's everyday experience (Galton, 1880a, b, 1883; Betts, 1909; Doob, 1972; Marks, 1972, 1999). A few people may insist that they rarely, or even never, consciously experience imagery (Galton, 1880a, 1883; Faw, 1997, 2009; but see Brewer and Schommer-Aikins, 2006), but for the vast majority of us, it is a familiar and commonplace feature of our mental lives. The English language supplies quite a range of idiomatic ways of referring to visual mental imagery: "visualizing," "seeing in the mind's eye," "having a picture in one's head," "picturing," "having/seeing a mental image/picture," and so on. There seem to be fewer ways to talk about imagery in other sensory modes, but there is little doubt that it occurs, and the experiencing of imagery in any sensory mode is often referred to as "imagining" (the appearance, feel, smell, sound, or flavor of something).[22]

Our ability to see is literal and figurative, in that our brains can generate images regardless of whether or not we are physically seeing an object with our eyes.

---

[22] "Mental Imagery," *Stanford Encyclopedia of Philosophy*, 2007.

David A. Wright, MD, MM, MBA, MHSA (Dr. David)

The ability to "see" without seeing, known as mental imagery, can be used as a way to improve athletic performance, to instill positive thinking, and to treat the symptoms of certain mental conditions. For example, the use of meditation to focus the mind on a single object can reduce the occurrence of intrusive thoughts in conditions such as OCD and ADHD. Though our general understanding of the ways in which mental imagery can affect us is pretty good, how and why we use it remain unanswered questions.[23]

There is plenty of research on imagery's effectiveness for a variety of issues. With regard to our bodies, this includes (but is not limited to) reducing the severity of hot flashes, postoperative pain and pain medication use; alleviating nausea; increasing mobility and decreasing pain in osteoarthritis, improving symptoms of asthma, and more. Imagery can also help alleviate stress and anxiety, improve self-confidence, help us visualize success, and enhance our ability to perform. Well-known athletes, including Tiger

---

[23] Kara Rogers, "Mental Imagery: The Power of the Mind's Eye," *Encyclopedia Britannica* blog, September 2008.

Woods, have been frank about their use of imagery to improve their games, and with good reason.[24]

Scientists have devised a way of reading your mind— or at least determining what you're looking at. By looking at your brainwaves, scientists at Stanford, Ohio State University and the University of Illinois at Urbana-Champaign are able to tell whether you're looking at a photo of a beach, cityscape, forest, highway, mountain or office, just by the pattern in which your neurons fire.

If brain space indicates the importance of a sense, then vision is the most important. Roughly 30 percent of neurons in the brain's cortex are devoted to vision, compared with 8 percent for touch, and 2 percent for hearing.

A genetic mutation found in approximately two to three percent of women allows them to see up to 100 million different colors—one hundred times

---

[24] Traci Stein, "7 Tips for Creating Positive Mental Imagery: How You Can Harness Your Imagination to Improve Your Body, Mind, and Life," *Psychology Today*, June 18, 2013.

more than the average person. Unlike other senses, human vision is processed in the back of the brain (in a location called the occipital lobe). The senses of smell, taste and hearing are processed in the sides of the brain (in the temporal lobes).

Researchers at the University of Pennsylvania have calculated that the human eye can transfer data at the rate of approximately 8.75 megabits per second— roughly triple the speed of the average Internet connection in the United States.

Scientists have found evidence that birds can literally see the earth's magnetic fields.[25]

"The ultimate purpose of the visual process is to arrive at an appropriate motor, and/or cognitive response."[26]

Although the visual processing mechanisms are not yet completely understood, recent findings from anatomical and physiological studies in monkeys

---

[25] "Beautiful Brains," *National Geographic*, November 22, 2011.

[26] Thomas Politzer, "Vision Is Our Dominant Sense," BrainLine, November 6, 2008.

suggest that visual signals are fed into at least three separate processing systems. One system appears to process information mainly about shape; a second, mainly about color; and a third, movement, location, and spatial organization. Human psychological studies support the findings obtained through animal research. These studies show that the perception of movement, depth, perspective, the relative size of objects, the relative movement of objects, shading, and gradations in texture all depend primarily on contrasts in light intensity rather than on color. Perception requires various elements to be organized so that related ones are grouped together. This stems from the brain's ability to group the parts of an image together and also to separate images from one another and from their individual backgrounds.[27]

Scientists at the Massachusetts Institute of Technology have discovered that an area of the brain previously thought to process only simple visual information also tackles complex images such as optical illusions. The research, conducted with animals, also provides

---

[27] "Vision: Processing Information," BrainFacts.org, April 21, 2012.

evidence that both the simple and more complex areas of the brain involved in different aspects of vision work cooperatively, rather than in a rigid hierarchy, as scientists have believed to date. "Because half of the human brain is devoted directly or indirectly to vision, understanding the process of vision provides clues to understanding fundamental operations in the brain," said Professor Mriganka Sur of MIT's Department of Brain and Cognitive Sciences. The research, which will appear in an issue of the journal *Science*, was conducted by Professor Sur, graduate student Bhavin R. Sheth, and postdoctoral fellows Jitendra Sharma and S. Chenchal Rao, all of the same department.[28]

Conclusions

Whenever you close your eyes and imagine something, your brain is creating, adjusting, or reinforcing your mental image of that thing and, in the process, is building the mental machinery (neurons, hormones, etc.) that are needed to help make that mental image a reality. And, yes, the images that you conjure up when you're stressed

---

[28] "Brain Processing of Visual Information," MIT News, MIT Research, MIT, December 19, 1996.

out, anxious, or scared will be created (just like the ones that you conjure up when you're peaceful, calm, content or happy).

However, don't take my word for it. In fact, don't take Einstein's, Walt Disney's, or any of the other authors' word for it.

Try this simple trick: Close your eyes and imagine one of the happiest moments of your life. Then look in the mirror, take a picture of your face, and notice how you feel.

Next, do the same thing, but this time think about one of the saddest or most painful moments of your life. Then look in the mirror, take a picture of your face, and notice how you feel.

Finally, think of one of the scariest moments in your life (when you experienced fear, such as arachnophobia, or had a near-death experience—or something else). Then look in the mirror, take a picture of your face, and notice how you feel.

What you should notice is that your expressions, feelings, and emotions, and other facets of your body and mind, will reflect the mental image that you've conjured up.

Interestingly enough, the same mental images that tend to imprison us (those relating to our fears, phobias, anxieties, etc.) also have the ability to set us free.

Do you use a vision board? Do you know someone who uses a vision board? Ever wonder why people use them or where they came from?

All thoughts, feelings, actions, behaviors, and human processes begin in the brain. You truly do have to see it in order to believe it, and you have to believe it in order to see it. Walt Disney said it best: "If you can dream it, you can do it."

Use visualizations in order to help you learn new things. Use visualizations and visual images to deconstruct complex processes and ideas to help you understand them. Use visualizations to change how you feel about your present or past circumstances. Use visualizations to fuel your dreams and future ambitions. Use visualizations to help ensure that you will start out your day on the right foot. Use visualizations and mental images to create the life that you desire. After all, when you combine a thought, a feeling, and an image, you can create *magic*.

Once you have begun to use the power of your greatest somatic (i.e., bodily) sense and its associated mind and brain connections to start to really craft the life that you desire, move on to the next chapter and start using a method that will allow you to permanently defeat procrastination and begin being more productive, efficient, and goal-directed than you've ever been before—using a simple system called the ROS!

CHAPTER 6

THE RANK ORDER SYSTEM (ROS) FOR ORGANIZATION (ESTABLISHING PRIORITIES AND MAKING DECISIONS)

Successful people learn, over time, not to become overwhelmed. They also learn what to do in the event they do become overwhelmed. One of the things they do is to go back to the basics. Another thing they do is to build in fail-safe systems to prevent becoming overwhelmed in the first place. Two basic skills that they develop, regardless of whether they choose to go back to the basics or build in fail-safe systems, are (1) to prioritize what they have to accomplish and (2) to make decisions logically, easily, and consistently. The rank order system (ROS) is a simple yet powerful method that I created (through working with my clients) that both prevents you from being overwhelmed and allows you to deal with being overwhelmed—through the use of two basic techniques that are prerequisites for being productive and efficient: (1) prioritization and (2) decision-making.

The absolute best method of not getting overwhelmed is to prevent being overwhelmed in the first place. However, the absolute best method of overcoming the sense of being overwhelmed after it has begun is to use the rank order system.

In the rank order system, first you're going to rank things that you need to get done based on their importance (i.e., the quality of the task). You'll assign everything that you have to do a number from 1 to 5 (with the most important tasks receiving a 1 and the least important tasks receiving a 5), with each task receiving a number based on its degree of importance compared to the other tasks on the list. As an example, college exam prep might receive a 1, whereas homework might receive a 3, and batting practice might receive a 5.

Then, you're going to rank things based on how soon they are due (i.e., temporal importance of the task). You'll assign everything that you have to do a second ranking based on the alphabet, from A to E, with A being the task that is due to be completed the soonest (i.e., something due within a few hours would be an A; something due the next morning might be an A or a B; and something due the following Monday might be a B or a C). Something that you have to constantly plan for but that might not occur for several months might receive a C, a D, or an E. So, if you're making the list in March, then you would assign a D to the task of creating a fall course schedule.

Then you combine the tasks and rank them. So, an A1 task would come first; an E5 would come last.

You should start mentally (i.e., in your mind) and physically (i.e., on paper), assigning a ranking to anything that you need to do, complete, or deliver (i.e., a task based on these criteria).

If you do get overwhelmed (such as if you have four important tasks and five minor tasks that have to be completed by Friday evening, and here it's Thursday morning), then go to your list and rank the tasks using this system. Then take a breath and get started with A1, A2, A3, A4, and A5, then B1, B2, B3, B4, and B5, and on and on until you're tired, until it's time for bed, or until you have to stop for some other reason. Then add the tasks that are left to the top of your to-do list for the next day.

Make a to-do list in three places: (1) in your mind as a mental note, (2) in your organizational notebook or pad, and (3) on your phone as a note or reminder.

Finally, if two or more items have the same ranking (e.g., there are two items that are C3), then use your gut instinct to choose which one to do first—or complete the task that is quickest and easiest first. If you continue to do this, then over time your mind will learn to gauge how to rank tasks more productively, efficiently, and accurately.

Once you have started using the rank order system to permanently defeat procrastination and to become more productive, efficient, and goal-directed than you've ever been before, begin to use the positive motivational quotations and inspiring, mindset-based inspirational self-affirmations in chapter 7 to begin permanently changing your thoughts, feelings, and belief systems.

CHAPTER 7

MOTIVATIONAL QUOTES, INSPIRATIONAL PHRASES, AND POSITIVE AFFIRMATIONS

Use this chapter to help empower you.

Use this chapter to help inspire you.

Use this chapter to help fuel your meditations.

Use this chapter to help fuel your dreams & aspirations.

Use this chapter to help fuel your hypnosis sessions.

Use this chapter to help energize your mind, body, spirit, soul & psyche.

Use this chapter to help you stay mentally refreshed and renewed.

Use this chapter in your thoughts and prayers.

Turn the Quotations into Positive Affirmations.

Turn the Statements & Phrases into "I" Statements & Affirmations.

This chapter is nourishment for your mind, body, spirit, soul & psyche.

Tear out your favorite pages & post them in prominent places where you will see them on a regular basis.

Add these phrases, quotations & affirmations to your daily vocabulary.

This Year, instead of going out and blowing all of your hard-earned money on buying more "STUFF" that you DON'T NEED and probably WON'T USE, make a DIFFERENT choice and invest in your own abundance, empowerment and prosperity!

Different OUTCOMES require Different CHOICES.

Invest where you're most likely to get the greatest return!

In general, Invest in YOURSELF, Your RELATIONSHIPS, & Your EXPERIENCES—Not in THINGS!

GRATITUDE is the Right Attitude for a Higher Altitude!

Just For today, "Accept Everyone and Everything"—devoid of any judgment.

Just For today, let things **BE**…

Trust me, you will have PLENTY of opportunities to JUDGE in the future!

Learning to be thankful will greatly empower you!

All that it requires are **PRACTICE** & **CONSISTENCY**.

Practice being THANKFUL consistently!

Each & every day, and in each & every way,

YOU have the POWER to choose & change your destiny!

Your TRAJECTORY is ONLY limited by your "Fortitude, Perseverance, Tenacity, Persistence, Ingenuity, Focus, Self-Control & Patience!"

You just have to keep pushing, refine your strategy, and plan for obstacles!

Keep Pushing, Keep Praying, Keep Meditating, & Keep DOING!

CHOOSE to CHANGE.

There's a *BIG* difference between "**HAVING Resources**" & "**BEING Resourceful!**"

Learn to be 'Specifically & Strategically' RESOURCEFUL.

You BECOME what you PRACTICE!

David A. Wright, MD, MM, MBA, MHSA (Dr. David)

PRACTICE "Suspending Judgment..."

You are what you PRACTICE!

Create SIMPLICITY.

SIMPLICITY is beautiful...

There's no time like the PRESENT to declutter your consciousness and your life!

SIMPLIFY.

DECLUTTER.

REPEAT...

MINIMALISM is "WINNABLEISM."

Your ONLY limitations are the ones in your own MIND!

Delete your limiting thoughts & beliefs, and install new ones that expand on who you are and what you can achieve!

"Hypnosis" & "Meditation" make it EASY!

You can do almost ANYTHING if you put your mind to it and create a STRATEGY!

You can accomplish ANYTHING that you can IMAGINE!

Test the LIMITS of your BELIEFS!

Your BELIEFS are the ONLY limits to your IMAGINATION!

Remember that lady who gave up???

EXACTLY.

No one else does either…

Don't Give Up!

And, get a support system around you that won't let you give up either!

Become RESILIENT!

Build some "Mental Muscles" that you didn't know that you had!

FIGHT for what you DESIRE!

FIGHT for what you SAY that you WANT!

FIGHT like there's NO TOMORROW!

FIGHT!

FIGHT on the INSIDE.

FIGHT on the OUTSIDE.

FIGHT!

Keep Fighting for what you DESIRE!

If there is one thing that I've learned in my 40+ years of living, extensive education and training, and professional experience is that PRACTICE makes PATHWAYS!

Whatever you practice on a daily basis is what you will be "**Designed To DO.**"

And, conversely, whatever you **DO** on a "Regular Basis" is a reflection of what you've been practicing.

Therefore, If you have habits, behaviors, actions and rituals that don't serve who you desire to be, then you have to "Unlearn & Un-practice" those behaviors (i.e., extinguish and delete them).

And, if there are habits, behaviors, actions and rituals that you'd like to have on a "Regular Basis", then you have to "Create, Install, & Practice" them CONSISTENTLY!

Make a "CONSCIOUS Choice" TODAY to do something "More Positive, More Productive & More Prudent" for your future self!

He or She will THANK YOU later on!

David A. Wright, MD, MM, MBA, MHSA (Dr. David)

Life is 10% the Present, and 90% Learning from History.

Learn from your PAST EXPERIENCES.

That's the ONLY WAY to prevent it from having been in vain…

Here's a Universal Principle: People will meet your needs and desires only to the extent that you meet theirs!

Contrary to popular opinion, rarely is love (or, anything else for that matter) UNCONDITIONAL.

Humans, and other Species of Animals, are "CONDITIONAL Creatures!"

We Sense, Think, Feel, Act, React, & Behave Based on CONDITIONS!

So, here's a Take-Home Lesson:
Give to others FIRST, BEFORE expecting something in return!

Give graciously & accept with gratitude!

God & the universe are NOT done with you or your harvest just yet...
Use the LAW OF ATTRACTION in order to create relationships that are CONGRUENT & COMPLIMENTARY to who you are and where you'd like your journey to go.

And, focus on the JOURNEY, not on the destination.

Here's a TIP for waking up on time or EARLY every morning: Before you go to sleep, picture a reward that you will receive the next morning. Picture it, smell it, taste it, feel it, and experience it. And, let yourself know that you will only receive it IF you wake up on time or early.

For example, my Anchor/Trigger is an Egg McMuffin. I smell, taste, and sense it and I tell myself that it's my reward. In fact, that's what I did this morning.

There are several KEY ingredients to this technique:

1. You have to create a mental image in your mind of both waking up early AND receiving the REWARD after you've accomplished that GOAL.

2. When you wake up early, then you have to provide yourself with that reward OR a with a better one.

3. The REWARD has to be something that you don't normally give or allow yourself. Examples might include a morning pastry, etc.

4. One super-duper assured way of using this technique is to pair it with music. So, download a new album from one of your favorite artists, and pair that with a pastry or treat that you

can enjoy on your way to work as you bask in the experience of arriving to work early.

5. As soon as you wake up, and as you drive to work enjoying your REWARDS, thank yourself multiple times.

David A. Wright, MD, MM, MBA, MHSA (Dr. David)

A bad day doesn't mean a bad life.

A tough day doesn't mean a tough life.

A hard moment doesn't mean a hard life.

Get Up, Get Over It, and Get MOVING!

Nourish yourself with empowerment so that the rough waves won't be so bad!

Nourish Your Cells with Nutrients.

Nourish Your Mind with Positive Thoughts.

Nourish Your Body with Relaxation & Rejuvenation.

Nourish Your Life with Friends and Family.

NOURISHMENT is the Key to CONTINUITY.

Your "Worst Journey" is the one that you never begin.

Your toughest part is the one that you keep avoiding.

Your best lesson is the one that keeps eluding you.

Face your FEARS!

Deal with your DEMONS!

Take accountability for what and whom you allow to influence you!

Who & what you allow to influence you matter MORE THAN ANYTHING ELSE!

CARE for the ENERGY that you carry with you!

VOTE.

Your Ancestors PAID the Ultimate Price for it!

See something NEW, each & every day!

See each day through a "NEW & IMPROVED" Lens of Life!

OPEN Your EYES to new & improved POSSIBILITIES & OPPORTUNITIES!

OPPORTUNITIES don't grow on trees...

POSSIBILITIES don't grow on vines...

It's up to YOU to CREATE them!

Don't live a life of "Open Doorways!"

Pick & choose [i.e., FILTER] what things and people you allow into your space, your environment, your life and your consciousness!

There's a reason why your coffee pot has a FILTER!

Can you imagine trying to enjoy a cup of coffee with all of those grindings floating around?

Create FILTERS in your life so that you can focus on what you do desire instead of dealing with the things that you don't desire...

Start creating the FILTERS needed in order to manifest YOUR HIGHEST DESTINY!

FILTER.

And filter carefully.

Stop allowing Just Anything & Absolutely Everything in!

Thoughts, CHOICES, Actions & DECISIONS are the Hallmarks of SUCCESS!

In order to change your circumstances and your outcomes,

you have to change your "Thinking, Actions, Behaviors, DECISIONS & CHOICES."

BETTER CHOICES & DECISIONS = BETTER RESULTS & OUTCOMES.

Most people don't make better CHOICES & DECISIONS on their own.

It takes either a monumental event in life, teaching/training/modeling, or BOTH...

Learn HOW to start thinking DIFFERENTLY and making CHOICES and strategic DECISIONS that are more in line with the DESTINY that you truly DESIRE!

It Starts with a **THOUGHT (or a FEELING)**, it Continues with a **CHOICE**, it Leads to an **ACTION**, and Ends with a **RESULT**.

Everything begins with an **IDEA**...

Just a **THOUGHT**.

Do you tend to have BLINDERS on in certain areas of your life?

If so, that's NOT a bad thing...

Just make sure that you have BLINDERS on for the "Right Types of Things" and NOT for the Wrong Ones.

BLINDERS & **BLINDS** are helpful, especially where negativity is concerned!

Do You have **"PAUSE" Buttons** in your life?

Some people call them "Hold Up, Wait a Minute!" Buttons.

"PAUSE", "PLAY", "STOP", "REWIND" & "RECORD" Buttons are ESSENTIAL for a balanced life!

Create BUTTONS for all occasions!

What illusions perpetuate in your mind, in your life, and in your world?

You are surrounded by them, constantly...

LIFE is all about PLANTING SEEDS.

And, the HARVEST begins with the **ROOTS**.

When You're UNCERTAIN, "Go Back to the BASICS."

Go back to the ROOTS...

Sometimes you have to Go Backward in order to Move Forward.

Patience PLUS Planning PLUS Persistence PLUS Perseverance is a Powerful Formula!

Preparation.

Planning.

Persistence.

Patience.

Practice.

Perseverance.

Proactivity.

Purpose.

Performance.

Productivity.

POWERFUL.

When in Need, Trust the Ps…

Do you trust what you See, Hear, Feel, Taste, Touch, &/or Think???

Do you trust your **GUT INSTINCTS?**

Is seeing really believing???

Do you have a VISION for the future?

Do you have to SEE it to believe it?

Not Sure???

Sometimes [Often Times] it's very difficult to "Think Outside of the Box" [i.e., "See Outside of the Circle", "Sense beyond the Sphere", etc.] when you're Part of the Packaging!

NEVER lose sight of your future plans, goals and ambitions!

And, do NOT allow temporary obstacles, dilemmas & challenges to obscure your view of your future possibilities!

Keep your EYES (i.e., your "I"s) on the GRAND PRIZE!

Turn Off your INNER CRITIC.

He/She never passed the background check!

Let's START Breaking Up Your Negative PATTERNS!

Interrupt the PATTERN.

Change the RITUAL.

Break the CYCLE.

Kill the HABIT.

Reverse the TREND.

End the STATUS QUO.

Dismantle the DESIGN.

Shift the CURRENT.

Crack the OSCILLATION.

Change The PARADIGM.

Evolve the STORYLINE.

One THOUGHT, One ACTION, & One BEHAVIOR at a TIME...

Your OUTCOMES begin with a single THOUGHT.

Start with ONE.

There's a Reason why it's the 1st Number!

Become a **WARRIOR** for Your Own Prosperity, Each & Every Day & in EVERY Way!

Become a **WARRIOR** for Your Happiness!

Become a **WARRIOR** for Your Mental Fitness!

Become a **WARRIOR** for Your Emotional Life!

Become a **WARRIOR** for Your Beginnings!

Become a **WARRIOR** for Your Integrity!

Become a **WARRIOR** for Your Empowerment!

Become a **WARRIOR** for Your Abundance!

Become a **WARRIOR** for YOURSELF & All of The Parts of YOU!

DEFEND Your PRESENT, and PROTECT Your FUTURE!

More & more people are choosing to invest in coaching, counseling and therapy these days.

However, you can TALK about your issues, dilemmas, problems and challenges with a counselor until the goats come home (or not), and the ONLY RESULT will be that you FEEL slightly better about the **VERY SAME PROBLEMS**.

TALKING alone will NOT change your trajectory.

Feeling better is a good thing, but if it's not followed by better results & outcomes then it will eventually lead to **DISAPPOINTMENT...**

Don't waste YEARS of your life TALKING about your problems & paying a counselor to sit there and listen to them (with minimal feedback or intervention)!

Choose a highly trained professional coach who will MAXIMIZE your investment & lead you on a path of TRANSFORMATION & EMPOWERMENT!

If you're not a REAL part of the PROCESS, then you're merely a BYSTANDER.

Take Accountability for Your WORDS.

Take Accountability for Your VOCABULARY.

Take Accountability for Your ACTIONS.

Take Accountability for Your REACTIONS.

Take Accountability for Your TIME.

Take Accountability for Your THOUGHTS.

Take Accountability for Your FEELINGS.

Take Accountability for Your MINDSET.

Take Accountability for Your FUTURE TRAJECTORY!

When you take accountability for the things that you say, feel, think, do & project to the world on a daily basis, then they become **A$$ET$** instead of **LIABILITIES!**

And, when you turn liabilities into A$$ET$, It will start to propel your personal life, your professional life, your financial life & your INCOME!

Start Turning Liabilities into A$$ETS!

Start Investing in your greatest potential A$$ET, YOURSELF!

All of Us, ALL OF US, in one way or (much more likely) in a multitude of ways, are operating on a daily basis on internal mental hardware and software that was designed between the ages of Birth and 10 years old.

That's one of the primary reasons WHY & HOW we seem to make the same mistakes over and over again--and, that's also HOW & WHY we have trouble breaking the very cycles that are preventing us from reaching our highest goals!

So, what's the solution? Well, of course, hardware and software updates!!!

Unlike machines, we have the ability to update our software and hardware ourselves—simply based on the NEED...

And, often times we do, especially as life forces us to grow, develop and mature.

But, it's those BLIND SPOTS that we all have that get in the way.

Don't allow aging cerebral hardware & obsolete mental software to prevent you from EVOLVING into the person whom you've always known that you could be.

Start upgrading your mental hardware & software so that it matches the world that we now live in and the changing goals that you desire to achieve in life!

PLAN for Slip-Ups!

They are a NORMAL Part of the CONTINUUM!

Slip-Ups prove that we're HUMAN...

The same interests & people who own the companies that produce the processed food products that are making everyone SICK also own the pharmaceutical companies that make the products that only help with the symptoms, fail to solve the underlying root causes, and also make you SICK...

It's Not a Conspiracy Theory.

It's an **ACTUAL Conspiracy** to get your money on a continuous basis!

Read BETWEEN The Lines...

VOTE.

Regardless of your ancestry, you should exercise your right to vote.

Even if you feel or think that it won't make a difference in your life, just remember that it may make a difference in the life of someone whom is less fortunate than you...

And, remember, you MOST LIKELY weren't always where you are today, financially, professionally, personally or otherwise...

Make certain that you are CURRENTLY registered to VOTE.

Don't Assume that you are still registered based on previous election cycles.

Know for SURE.

Make VOTING a PRIORITY instead an Afterthought!

VOTE.

If not for yourself, for someone else (like your children)...

Claim TODAY as Your Day to Succeed.

Claim TODAY as Your Day to Do Something DIFFERENT.

Claim TODAY as Your Day to Propel Your Trajectory.

Claim TODAY as Your Day to Take a Calculated Risk.

Claim TODAY as Your Day to Do, Think & Be BETTER.

Claim & Proclaim TODAY.

NOT TOMORROW...

TODAY!

Stop Trying to be ALL THINGS to ALL PEOPLE.

Pick a few things and a few people…

Don't be a jack of all trades and a master of NONE!

Choose QUALITY over QUANTINTY, Every Single Time, Time after Time!

You Don't Have to be Your PAST.

You Don't Have to be What Happened to You.

You Don't Have to be Defined by Negative Past Experiences.

You Don't Have to React Based on Past Tragedies.

You Don't Have to Represent Your Baggage.

You Don't Have to Carry the Weight of Your Struggle.

You DO Get to Break Through Stagnation.

You DO Get to Discard The Baggage that has held you Back for so long.

You DO Get to Reset the Tone of Your LIFE.

You DO Get to Evolve into what You Were DESIGNED To BE.

You DO GET TO REDEFINE Today & Tomorrow!

However, It doesn't Happen AUTOMATICALLY...

Self-Actualization & Self-Determination **DON'T** happen by Accident, and neither does FAILURE.

They're both due to the presence or absence of Thoughts, Actions & Strategies!

Self-Determination Requires a Definitive, Strategic, Calibrated PROCESS!

There are NO ACCIDENTS.

Don't live a life based on them...

It all Starts & Ends with the **BASICS: INPUT = OUTPUT.**

You ARE your DIET!!!

You ARE what you CONSUME.

Everything that you See, Hear, Feel, Experience, Think, and Manifest relate DIRECTLY to your DIET!

If you put in JUNK, that's exactly what you'll get in RETURN...

If you feel like crap, it's because that's what you've been eating.

Make Change, Growth & Evolution CORE parts of who you are, what you do, and how you operate on a Daily Basis...

Small changes lead to BIGGER changes.

Small & big changes combine to create LEAPS in TRANSFORMATION!

Change a little bit for the BETTER, each & every day!

Strengthen your CORE… Your MENTAL CORE.

David A. Wright, MD, MM, MBA, MHSA (Dr. David)

Getting Up (or Getting Back Up) is HALF the BATTLE!

Get Up & Get Going!

Get to **GOING**.

Get to **ACTING**.

Get to **THINKING**.

Get to **DOING**.

Get go **BEING**!

Try not to LABEL.

You never know, your blessings might be disguised within LABELS with which you might not readily identify...

That's WHY they are called sometimes called "Blessings in Disguise."

David A. Wright, MD, MM, MBA, MHSA (Dr. David)

Make SMALL, but CONCERTED changes every single day!

Small things have a way of GROWING!

Small CHANGES.

If You can't make SMALL changes,

then what makes you think that you can make BIG changes???

SMALL WINS are Life Changing!

A SINGLE THOUGHT has the POWER to Change Your DESTINY.

Thoughts MATTER.

Don't underestimate the POWER OF A SINGLE THOUGHT!

Planting a THOUGHT is Just Like Planting a SEED.

After it has been planted all that it needs is fertile ground, energy, nourishment, time & attention!

Eventually, with Consistency of Care, It will lead to a HARVEST!

Use today to recreate prosperity & abundance in your life by **RESETTING Your MINDSET & PLANTING Some Positive THOUGHTS!!!**

Think **BETTER.**

Act **BETTER.**

Behave **BETTER.**

Eat **BETTER.**

Live **BETTER.**

Do **BETTER.**

Feel **BETTER.**

Get **BETTER.**

Be **BETTER.**

You are BETTER!

Re-invent what you Say, Think, & DO on a Consistent, Habitual Basis!

You can only do that by pushing, expanding, and stretching what currently constrains you!

In other words, in order to GROW…
You have to Continuously & Consistently Challenge your own limitations!

Take an active approach & plan towards **SIMPLICITY** in your life!

Although life can throw you a lot of curve balls, DO take the time to get your life back on track to what is easily managed!

SIMPLIFY.

START creating an environment geared towards empowerment, success & prosperity!

Start molding your environment in ways that promote what you DESIRE!

DO make heart-healthy, fresh fish a consistent component of your weekly diet.

You will look & feel better!

Your BODY will thank you!

Frequently Feast on Fresh Fish!

Life is about THOUGHTS, FEELINGS, EMOTIONS, WORDS, ACTIONS & BEHAVIORS.

You can pray all day, every day, and it still won't get you to where you'd like to be UNLESS you take **ACTION**.

ACTIONS do speak LOUDER than words.

And, they tend to produce more noticeable and quantifiable results too!

But, the combination of thoughts, feelings, words, actions & behaviors that reinforce your altitude is the greatest strategy for reaching your goals!

God programmed you with the Tools to ACT & DO!

Use them!

Start Taking ACTION in All Areas of Your Life!

Your **TIME** is one of your greatest assets!

Use It, or Lose It!

Believe it or not, **TIME is MONEY.**

If you're not Maximizing Your TIME, then You're Losing Your MONEY!

Self-Care & Self-Efficacy are the **FOUNDATIONS** of Self-Esteem & Self Confidence!

Self-Care is Your Duty.

Self-Efficacy is Your Responsibility.

Self-Esteem is Your Right.

Self-Confidence is Your Gift.

Your Heart, Mind, Body, Soul, Spirit & Psyche were GIFTS!

Treat them as such!

Find solutions to your own, inner dilemmas,

and the mountains before you will begin to crumble...

The "True Path", as well as the "True Answers", reside where they've

always been, right inside of YOU!

If you invest in solving the riddles WITHIN,

then the puzzles OUTSIDE won't seem so mysterious!

Refuse to confront your own demons, and watch them lead you to (or,

keep you in) a place of complacency, stagnation, & disappointment...

Begin the process of solving your own riddles, challenges, & dilemmas

in ways that will allow you to become RESILIENT!

Make PROGRESS, Not EXCUSES.

Progress Leads to SUCCESS.

Excuses Lead to FAILURE.

Choose PROGRESS.

Make a **CHOICE**.

Take excellent care of your thoughts.

They are the keys to your DESTINY!!!

Thoughts matter, MORE than you know...

A SINGLE THOUGHT has the POWER to ALTER Your DESTINY!

Exercise COMPASSION in your dealings, communications & relationships!

COMPASSION isn't just about solutions!

COMPASSION is also about the ENERGY that you create, manifest, share, and exchange with others!

Become a TRADER of POSITIVE ENERGY.

Start with COMPASSION.

Don't allow others to create (or curse) your reality!

Create, manifest, perpetuate & evolve your very own reality!

Don't take a PASSIVE role in your own PLAY!

Don't be a bit player in your own prosperity!

Perfection is an ILLUSION!

Go for Wholeness, Balance, Abundance, Empowerment, Prosperity & BLISS Instead.

When you're READY to begin creating BLISS in your life, then you'll give up your quest for perfection.

It's NOT all that it's cracked up to be.

The BEST WAY to "Predict the Future" is to CREATE IT!

Steve Jobs also embraced that Concept!

So, I ask you, what are you DOING & BEING to CREATE your own future?

Do you do something specific EACH & EVERY day to make it more probable that the future that you inherit is one that you actually intentionally & strategically created based on your own desires?

Healing spreads, just like everything else!

Let your healing empower someone else...

It will come back to you!

Don't be too proud or too ashamed to share your story!

After all, you've already PAID for it!

If you desire to become SUCCESSFUL,

Then DO be willing to DO what others aren't willing to DO!

What you are and/or aren't willing to do has one of the greatest degrees of influence over your ability to become SUCCESSFUL!

DO what others won't DO in order to ACHIEVE what others won't ACHIEVE!

Strength, coupled with Tenderness and Mercy, is a powerful combination!

It's a RECIPE for **CHARACTER**.

Take ACTION!

Stay In MOTION!

Keep CREATING!

Continue MANIFESTING!

Start REVISING & RE-EVALUATING!

THINK, FEEL, CREATE, DO, MANIFEST, REVISE & REPEAT!!!

USE the verbs & language of EMPOWERMENT in your life consistently!

FEAR & ANXIETY (The body's responses to FEAR) have the greatest ability to prevent you from reaching your highest level of potential (i.e., SUCCESS).

If you learn to embrace and manage them, then you can Conquer The World!

If You don't, then you'll never reach your highest potential.

It's THAT Simple.

Don't Give FEAR a VOTE in the Greatest Election of Your Life!

Remember the Wizard of Oz?

COURAGE is a Psychological, Emotional & Mental Muscle, Just Like Tenacity, Determination, Self-Control, Perseverance, Fortitude and Self Confidence!

You have to USE it in order to GROW It!

Walk Through INSECURITY in order to reach COURAGE…

And, Start Growing & Building Your Own Mental Muscles!

Constantly re-Invent yourself NOT by becoming someone else,

but by maximizing your strengths & minimizing your weaknesses!

Take strategic action towards becoming the best version of YOU!

It's NOT about being a chameleon,

It's about EVOLVING emotionally, psychologically and otherwise.

And becoming BETTER!

Start with BETTER.

Use your physiology in order to change your mentality.

And, use your mentality to change your physiology...

Create BALANCE using all of the tools at your disposal.

Most processes in life are not unidirectional.

Become a CREATER!

Learn to CREATE!

It doesn't matter what it is, just start creating something POSITIVE.

The more that you create, the more that comes back to you!

But, don't take my word for it...

Just Ask Oprah Winfrey!

What has she created, and what has come back to her?

She's the queen of creating positivity & transformation!

The math is clear [and, easy]...

Consciously & strategically create Joy, Happiness, Abundance, Empowerment, Contentment, Bliss & Prosperity within Your LIFE!

Don't leave anything as important as those things to Accident, Chance or Happenstance...

CREATE On PURPOSE.

If you are strategic about creating a family, career, social life, etc., then why wouldn't you do the same with the joy, happiness, abundance, empowerment, contentment & prosperity [i.e., BALANCE & HARMONY] that you desire in your life?

Care for your ENERGY, both going OUT and coming IN.

Your ENERGY directs your TRAJECTORY!

Account for your own ENERGY!

Actively, creatively, & INTENTIONALLY create, develop and manifest who you ARE!

Let it be a process of which you are in control, instead of you becoming someone whom you don't want to be by accident...

The Worst Disability is a Bad Attitude.

David A. Wright, MD, MM, MBA, MHSA (Dr. David)

POSITIVELY change lives in MONUMENTAL ways!

TENACITY, RESILIENCE, FORTITUDE & PERSEVERANCE are the "TRUE", Time-Tested KEYS to SUCCESS!!!

But, they are MUSCLES!

You have to BUILD, STRETCH & CONDITION them regularly!

A little bit of SPUNK never hurt either...

David A. Wright, MD, MM, MBA, MHSA (Dr. David)

Your IMAGINATION is one of your greatest GIFTS!

Don't neglect it!

Because, it will never desert you!

IMAGINE the reality that you DESIRE to create!

Return to your TRUE self!

I assure you that it's still there, hidden and buried beneath all of the dust, cobwebs and baggage from the past...

Return to Your ROOTS!

Schedule an Occasional Visit, at the least.

Mediocrity is NOT your DESTINY!

Strive to be the BEST YOU possible!!!

Don't settle for Mediocrity.

And, please don't be "BASIC."

Don't be the Lowest Common Denominator [i.e., the LCD] in your own life!

PEACE deserves & requires a PLAN, just like everything else does...

What is your PEACE PLAN?

What You EARN represents & reflects parts of you!

If Your Income is STAGNANT, Then it's possible that your personal & professional growth are stagnant as well—Since what you earn is a projection of them...

If you want your INCOME to increase, then parts of you have to increase [i.e., Grow, Evolve, Mature & Multiply].

The BEST, FASTEST way to GROW your INCOME is to GROW YOURSELF!

Listen To Oprah Winfrey's Words of Wisdom:

Do what you enjoy & love, Do It Well, and the MONEY will come...

Invest in Yourself, and Have Faith in Your Works!

BALANCE is The KEY!

And, sometimes BALANCE will require you to give up some things and some individuals in order to allow room for others!

It's literally IMPOSSIBLE to gain positive elements
when you're unwilling to let go of negative elements
—Even if those negative elements are familiar, safe and time tested...

Be willing to let go of the familiar in order to allow for something BETTER & MORE FULFILLING!

It's the BEST way to GROW!

And, It Requires BALANCE!

Let's Check your BALANCE!

No one wants an account that's OVERDRAWN!

David A. Wright, MD, MM, MBA, MHSA (Dr. David)

Have FAITH When It COUNTS, Not Just When It's CONVENIENT!

Forgiveness is one of the greatest gifts that you can give to others, and to yourself!

Use it Wisely, and Often...

There are no FAILURES.

There is only FEEDBACK.

Learn from the FEEDBACK, but don't interpret it as a FAILURE.

"Feedback & Experiences" are **OPPORTUNITIES** to get it right the next time around.

MOST THINGS THAT HAPPEN IN LIFE DON'T OCCUR BY ACCIDENT, THEY HAPPEN BY DESIGN, ON PURPOSE, & FOR A SPECIFIC REASON!

Here's something to think about: The Opioid Epidemic in this country was not by ACCIDENT. It was 100%, Completely & Absolutely by DESIGN.

I'm sure there are animal models, experiments and trials out there showing some poor animal endlessly pressing on a lever or tapping a button to get another delivery of a narcotic... They Knew that from DAY ONE!

Here's something even greater to think about: ALL of the things out there that people get addicted to are by DESIGN! Every Single One of them...

Moral of the Story: Create a System in Your Life that Pro-Actively Prevents You from Getting Addicted to things that aren't and won't be Good for You in the LONG-TERM!

PRO-ACTIVITY & PROACTIVENESS Prevent RE-ACTIVITY & REACTIVENESS!

David A. Wright, MD, MM, MBA, MHSA (Dr. David)

You Are ENERGY!

ENERGY is the ability to do work!

And, good works lead to ACCOMPLISHMENTS!

Therefore, you are the ability to ACCOMPLISH!

Choose TODAY to start taking control of what entities you allow
to contribute to or take away from your own energy!

Take Control of what allows you to be happy or not!

If you fail to take control of the levers and pulleys that facilitate your happiness, then others will do it for you!

And, I guarantee you that you won't be Happy with the OUTCOME!

Otherwise, you're just an ADDICT...

Delete the Mental Buttons that don't serve your highest goals.

Take control of your thoughts, feelings, emotions & your DEEDS [i.e., **ACTIONS**]!

They are the greatest **A$$ETS** that You Have, Literally & Figuratively!

WHAT you think & feel and HOW you respond to the world [i.e., **REACTIONS**] literally controls HOW much money you make!

Don't Believe Me? Just Watch Oprah on Super Soul Sundays!

Don't allow the world around you to turn your gifts into **LIABILITIES**!

Start taking Accountability for both the Causes & Effects in your life!

Do What You Care About, & Care About What You Do.

David A. Wright, MD, MM, MBA, MHSA (Dr. David)

You are "ENOUGH!"

But, don't let that stop you from Being "MORE!"

Start doing & becoming "MORE."

You are MORE.

Become MORE.

Be MORE.

What is your HEALING PLAN?

What is your plan for repairing your emotional & psychological scars?

Why Bother?

Because, once you begin to HEAL, Then you will start to manifest "Abundance, Empowerment & Prosperity" within your "Spheres of Living" in ways that you never could have imagined!

Begin the HEALING PROCESS!

You & All Of the Parts of You Deserve It!

Anyone who shoots a dolphin or a protected species should go to prison!

Some people have no class & absolutely no decency...

One Word?

KARMA.

Errors, Mistakes, Accidents, Disappointments and

Unexpected, Non-Positive Outcomes are NOT Failures!

They are Opportunities to Learn, Improve & Gain **EXPERIENCE!**

In Fact, Most Successful Individuals have "FAILED"

thousands to millions of times BEFORE they have succeeded!

Infants FAIL thousands of times as they attempt to walk,

but Each and Every Time they get back up and "Try It Again."

They don't view their lack of success on any given attempt as a

"FAILURE."

And, They don't INTERNALIZE it either.

We can Learn a Lot from Them!

Start Looking at Your "Perceived" Shortcomings as FEEDBACK

instead of FAILURE.

David A. Wright, MD, MM, MBA, MHSA (Dr. David)

Don't Settle for Normal, Regular, Average, Mediocre or BASIC!

Strive for the BEST!

And, Don't Allow Others to Improperly Influence You Into NORMALITY!

Begin Your Journey Out of NORMALITY & BASICITY!

Create & practice OPTIMISM until It becomes Habit, Routine, Ritual, & NORMAL!

Because, Whether you realize it or not, PESSIMISM was practiced until it became Habit, Routine, & Ritual TOO!

Create & Practice OPTIMISM.

It has the Power to Transform the PLANET!

A Strong Partnership DIVIDES the Effort and MULTIPLIES the Effect.

—John Maxwell

SUCCESS Is NO ACCIDENT!

SUCCESS comes from a STRATEGY!

You need a STRATEGY!

Re-Train Your brain to see Disappointments, Challenges, Obstacles, Problems, Mistakes, Errors, & Dilemmas as Opportunities & Experiences!!!

And, you MUST have a strategy!

Winging it alone or on Auto-Pilot won't work!

Start retraining your brain & mind for IMPROVEMENT & SUCCESS instead of allowing them to run on Autopilot towards Complacency, Mediocrity & FAILURE!

Dolly Parton got it Right!

You're Very First & Most Important Job In LIFE is getting to Know, Understand, Acknowledge, Appreciate & Become Comfortable with Yourself!

—Dolly Parton

Your Second Job is to Improve Upon Yourself!

And, Your Third Job is to Improve Upon Others!

However, Very Few Of Us Really Take the Time to Get to Truly Know Ourselves.

And, That's Why we Get & Feel "STUCK."

David A. Wright, MD, MM, MBA, MHSA (Dr. David)

OWN Your Own Existence, Before Someone Else Does!!!

Setting Boundaries in Your Life will SAVE You Thousands of Dollars & Lots of Disappointments, Frustrations & Heartaches!

Don't believe me? Talk with a Group of Millionaires about Boundary Setting?

Are you Ready to Start Setting Boundaries in Both Your Personal & Professional Lives that Ensure that you Reach Your Goals, Visions & Ambitions?

You have to Protect Your Goals, Visions, & Ambitions from a Crazy world that is Designed to Destroy Them.

When was the last time that you took the Time to Clean Your Consciousness?

When was the last time that you took the Time to Clean Your Subconscious Mind?

Do you know HOW to do Either?

Here's a HINT: It starts with Hypnosis, Introspection & Meditation.

Are You RESOURCEFUL???

HOW Do You Recognize Opportunities in Your LIFE?

WHEN Do You Seize Options for Empowerment?

WHAT Resources Do You Have Ready Access To?

WHOM in Your Life Do You Use as a Positive Resource?

WHY Are Resources Important?

You need to be able to Answer all of these questions if you want to be on a Pathway towards Abundance, Empowerment, Prosperity & Success!

What is the Status of Your SOUL???

WHAT do you feed It?

HOW do you nurture it?

WHEN do you check its status?

You need to be able to answer all of these questions if you want to be on a Pathway towards Abundance, Empowerment Happiness & Prosperity!

Use a Specific Strategy to Seize Every Moment of Your Day!

And, the Strategy Has To Be SPECIFIC to YOU, Who You are, Where You are, and Where You'd Like to Go...

In Essence, Your Strategy Determines Your Journey
—And, Your Journey Determines Your Destiny.

But, It all starts with a STRATEGY!

Using Someone Else's Strategy will NOT Work for YOU!

It's THEIR Strategy, Not YOURS...

Work Hard.

Exercise Due Diligence.

Do Persevere Through & Beyond Adversities.

Always Make Adjustments to Your Planning & Strategy as You Receive Feedback & Make Progress...

But NEVER, EVER Give Up!

It is through helping others discover who they are that you discover who you are.

And, "That" JOURNEY is your "Real" EDUCATION.

IF You Desire to live an Abundant, Empowered & Prosperous LIFE, then you can't afford to choose between what's on the inside and what's on the outside...

You Have To Work on BOTH, Simultaneously!

They are inexorably INTERTWINED.

OUTER Simplicity & Order bring about INNER Calm & Tranquility.

Order & Simplify your affairs.

David A. Wright, MD, MM, MBA, MHSA (Dr. David)

You have CHOICES, OPPORTUNITIES & OPTIONS.

SEIZE the ones that you can control, and use them WISELY.

Motivational Quotes, Inspirational Phrases, and Positive Affirmations

Your IMAGINATION is a PREVIEW of What's Coming Up Next.

David A. Wright, MD, MM, MBA, MHSA (Dr. David)

Every Single Day is a New Opportunity to SUCCEED!

Seize EVERY SINGLE Day!

Carpe Diem!

Become responsible for your experience of LIFE!

I guarantee you that no one else will volunteer for the job...

Ultimately, you're Responsible for your own Experiences.

IF you reasonably expect to succeed at something,

Then you have to have a STRATEGY.

The degree to which you take care of yourself

determines the degree to which you are able to manifest your desires...

Hence, if you don't take care of yourself, then you won't manifest

Abundance, Empowerment & Prosperity within your LIFE!

It goes back to a BASIC CONCEPT:

In order to draw a RETURN, then you have to make an INVESTMENT!

So, What is your STRATEGY for Taking Care of Yourself?

INCARCERATION Is NOT by ACCIDENT...

It's Totally by DESIGN.

It's a Modern Incarnation [or, INCARCERATION] of our Nation's History.

Just because you weren't around during the planning doesn't mean there isn't a design.

What is HAPPINESS???

What is JOY??

What is ABUNDANCE??

What is EMPOWERMENT???

What is PROSPERITY CONSCIOUSNESS???

How can You Achieve them and Create Success in Your LIFE???

The Journey Starts with **QUESTIONS**, Not ANSWERS.

Motivational Quotes, Inspirational Phrases, and Positive Affirmations

Aspire, Respire, Conspire, & Inspire Positive Energy.

Yes, It's ALL ABOUT **"SPIRING."**

Nothing in LIFE is FREE.

Nothing Worthwhile is FREE...

If it's worthwhile, then it has a VALUE, and if it has a VALUE, then it is NOT Free.

Just because you aren't the one who has to PAY FOR it doesn't mean that it's FREE...

That simply means that SOMEONE ELSE has/had to pay for it.

Nothing of VALUE is FREE.

Is the Glass Half Empty or Half Full?

You have that CHOICE about Everything in life...

MINDSET Matters.

Learn from Your Mistakes...

Don't DWELL on them, but Don't DENY them either.

Observe & Notice Them, Analyze Them & Allow Them to Improve You & Your Circumstances!

EVERYBODY Needs HELP or ASSISTANCE at SOME Point...

DON'T Be Too Proud to Ask for a Helping Hand!

Just make sure that the Hand that you ask for is capable of HELPING...

David A. Wright, MD, MM, MBA, MHSA (Dr. David)

You ARE.

You DO.

And, You BELONG Here...

Don't Give Up!

Never Give Up!

Keep Pushing Forward!

There are Helping Hands in places that you can't see…

David A. Wright, MD, MM, MBA, MHSA (Dr. David)

You Don't have to be PERFECT in order to Be ACCOUNTABLE...

How do you begin to install new empowerment programs
in your mind and in your life?

Think it.

Say it.

See it.

Do it.

Believe it.

Live it.

Become it.

REPEAT IT.

If You Desire LOVE, Then the EASIEST & Most ASSURED Way of getting it is to GIVE it FIRST!!!

Be The FIRST.

Take Control of the OUTCOME!

Don't be FOOLED!

WEED is NOT just a Harmless Plant—Especially If It's Bought Off of the Street.

David A. Wright, MD, MM, MBA, MHSA (Dr. David)

Tell Your Past: Thank You!

Tell Your Present: I'm with You!

Tell Your Future: Here I come! I've been PLANNING to meet you!

BITTERNESS is the Seed of MISERY.

Forgive & Forget.

David A. Wright, MD, MM, MBA, MHSA (Dr. David)

Create & Manifest Your VALUE...

Then, Know & Understand Your VALUE!

Don't, however, Underestimate or Overestimate Your VALUE.

Define your VALUE.

Stop GUESSING about it!

Turn Your Suffering into Grace, Temperance & Mercy.

Learn to Transform Your Experiences into WISDOM.

TIME can be Your Greatest ASSET, or it can be Your Worst LIABILITY...

If you want TIME, Then You Have to Make TIME.

In order to Make TIME, You Have to Plan TIME.

In order to Plan TIME, You have to have a STRATEGY...

Create a PLAN.

Start with a STRATEGY.

Continue with a JOURNEY.

End with ASSETS!

Don't focus on either just the OUTSIDE or just the INSIDE.

Focus on BOTH and help them to meet one another in the middle.

Don't be Fooled Into Faulty Choices & Silly Dichotomies!

You can Choose MORE THAN ONE Option.

Create Your Own MENU.

David A. Wright, MD, MM, MBA, MHSA (Dr. David)

Keep Dreaming!

And, Keep DOING!

RINSE & REPEAT!!!

Do You TRUST Yourself?

If You Don't TRUST Yourself, Then HOW Can You Expect Others to TRUST Your Words or Actions?

Learn to TRUST Yourself...

It takes PRACTICE.

Challenges, Experiences & Practices create TRUST.

Don't Confuse Your Individual STEPS with Your Master PLAN...

There's the BIG PICTURE, and there are Individual PIXELS.

They all MATTER.

You ARE Your OUTCOMES & RESULTS, as a Result of Your CHOICES...

Desire Different OUTCOMES, Then Make Different CHOICES!

It Begins with a DESIRE.

It Continues with a CHOICE.

It Manifests into a DECISION.

It Creates a JOURNEY.

And It Ends with an OUTCOME or a RESULT.

David A. Wright, MD, MM, MBA, MHSA (Dr. David)

"Self-Esteem", "Self-Confidence", "Self-Appraisal" & "Self-Empowerment"

are the UNDERPINNINGS & FOUNDATIONS of SUCCESS!!!

You have to SHOW UP in order to GROW UP!!!

And, You have to GROW UP to SHOW UP!!!

Believe it or not, the *Chicken and the Egg came at the same time*!

Your Story has NOT Been Told Yet.

So, STOP Dropping the Pen.

Keep Writing.

TREASURE your loved ones while they are here...

TOMORROW isn't promised.

And, TODAY is NOT Guaranteed.

David A. Wright, MD, MM, MBA, MHSA (Dr. David)

Everything that Happens, Happens for a Reason & In a Season...

However, You Gain SO MUCH MORE by focusing Not Just on the Reason, or on The Result—But, On The Interaction between the TWO!!!

It's Not Just the What, the Why, the When, or the HOW...

It's ALL Of Them, and HOW They Interact!

Think Multifactorially & Multidimensionally...

Use ALL of Your 6 Thinking HATS!

Embrace ALL of the Shades of GREY!

That's Where 99% of Things Exist & Occur!

It's Not Just What You THINK, It's Not Just What You SAY, & It's Not Just What You DO...

It's What You BECOME and INSPIRE in Others that Also Matter.

Dare to EVOLVE!

David A. Wright, MD, MM, MBA, MHSA (Dr. David)

Take a CHANCE on YOU!!!

In order to RECEIVE Love, you have to First GIVE Love...

Ask, and you shall receive...

Give, and you shall receive even MORE!

David A. Wright, MD, MM, MBA, MHSA (Dr. David)

DARE to Dream,

DARE to Create,

DARE to Manifest!!!

Don't Be AFRAID to Take Considered, Calculated Risks...

NOTHING Ventured, NOTHING Gained.

Focus on What you DESIRE, Not on What you FEAR.

FEAR is a Mind killer.

Do NOT FEAR.

David A. Wright, MD, MM, MBA, MHSA (Dr. David)

Everything Counts in Different Amounts!!!

Pay Special Attention to the things that SHOULD Count in Large Amounts...

They aren't always OBVIOUS.

Be There.

Be There for YOU!!!

Show up for Yourself FIRST.

You Have to Think It, See It, Believe It, & DO It in order to make it HAPPEN!!!

It begins with a THOUGHT, and it continues with an ACTION, And it ends with an OUTCOME/RESULT.

Make it HAPPEN...

Think...

DO!

Be.

Trust the Process as You Create It.

Which really means "TRUST YOURSELF."

David A. Wright, MD, MM, MBA, MHSA (Dr. David)

PAY IT FORWARD!

Not Because You'll Automatically Get it Right Back, But Because of what you CREATE (and, who you BECOME) when you do so...

SOUND & MUSIC have the Power to CHANGE Your STORY!!!

They SPEAK Feelings that can't be described in words.

David A. Wright, MD, MM, MBA, MHSA (Dr. David)

IF you want to Open NEW DOORS,

Then Stop Using the Same OLD KEYS...

Upgrade Your KEYS!!!

Waking UP & Getting Started is 90% of the BATTLE...

Start DOING!

Begin BEING!

Think. Then Do.

Review.

Think. Then Do.

Review.

REPEAT.

Think, Feel, Do & Review.

REPEAT.

Society won't get any better on its own.

It's up to US...

ALL of US.

David A. Wright, MD, MM, MBA, MHSA (Dr. David)

Your WORK is NEVER in vain...

The rewards may just not have had ample time to materialize and reveal themselves.

NEVER Give Up!!!

There are a MILLION words for it,

But they ALL mean the same thing: Don't EVER Give Up!

Every SECOND is an OPPORTUNITY to CREATE!!!

Create & Embrace the Future, Enjoy & Live the Present, but NEVER Forget the Past...

Occasionally, HISTORY teaches us Powerful Lessons about ourselves.

David A. Wright, MD, MM, MBA, MHSA (Dr. David)

ACCOUNTABILITY is a STRATEGY!

You have to LEARN & PRACTICE it...

Be Deliberate!

You Choose!

Instead of allowing others to choose FOR You...

David A. Wright, MD, MM, MBA, MHSA (Dr. David)

Don't Be Ashamed to Go after what you Desire in LIFE...

Simply make sure that you go about it the "RIGHT" Way.

SUCCESS Doesn't happen by Accident.

It's manifested through Consistent Planning, Strategy, & Execution...

Perfection is NOT possible.

However, WHOLENESS is within your reach...

Seek, Find, Discover, & Create Wholeness in Your Life.

Life if FULL of Opportunities & Possibilities...

Opportunities are Merely Possibilities that haven't been Appropriately Realized & Appreciated.

Opportunities are Possibilities that have yet to Materialize...

All that you have to do to become more successful is to learn to see the possibilities & create the opportunities...

It's that SIMPLE.

But, you have to have a STRATEGY.

You have to become a STRATEGY.

You have to Start "THINKING" & "FEELING" it

in order to "ACT ON" and "CREATE" it...

It all Starts with 1 Thought, 1 Feeling;

Followed by 1 ACTION!

Your Support Network of Family & Friends is

TRULY the Most Valuable Commodity that you have...

Don't forget to use it, and be available as a resource to your

Family & Friends when they need you!

And, When you need Help, ASK For It!!!

NOTHING That was Built to Last was created and maintained

Singularly...

LIFE is All About CONNECTIONS!

Think, Feel, Exude, Show, & Illustrate SUCCESS!!!

Yes, you have to do that BEFORE you receive it...

You ARE "Enough"!!!

You are MORE THAN "Enough"!!!

Now, It's Time for you to start acting like and treating yourself like you are "WORTHY" & "OF VALUE."

Don't EVER forget who you ARE!!!

And, Allow Your Inner Child to Explore, Experiment, and Grow in NEW Ways...

Don't Go it Alone!

Start Creating & Manifesting Your EQ instead of just relying on your IQ!

Create Your Own Winning Team!

Everyday, In Every Way, Remind Yourself
that [even while becoming greater] you ARE ENOUGH!!!

You are "MORE THAN" Enough!

When You CAN, TRY to "Pay It Forward."

It WILL come back to you, sooner or later, one way or another...

It's True: What goes around comes around, and what comes around goes around...

David A. Wright, MD, MM, MBA, MHSA (Dr. David)

Find the BALANCE between Doing it ALL (i.e., Being a Superhero)

and Doing Nothing at ALL (i.e., Complacency & Stasis)!

More Than Anything Else, Be WILLING & OPEN to

using your Support System to help you through the Tough Times...

Don't forget to do the Not-So-Little Things!

They're PRICELESS!!!

David A. Wright, MD, MM, MBA, MHSA (Dr. David)

Procrastination is a Success Killer...

But, It's NEVER Too Late to Re-Begin any Journey!

You Are ENOUGH!!!

But, it's NOT Enough to Simply Say it...

You have to start THINKING, DOING, BEING, PRACTICING & LIVING it!!!

It takes a VILLAGE!

Don't Go it ALONE...

David A. Wright, MD, MM, MBA, MHSA (Dr. David)

You May not realize it, but You're a Gardener...

So am I!

We all are to some extent.

Each and Every one of Us were created to be ENOUGH!

So, be mindful of what you plant, how your nourish it,

and when it's time for harvest...

We're all part of the Cycle of Growth and the Circle of Life!

You only live ONCE, but if you do it RIGHT, Once is ENOUGH.

—Mae West

David A. Wright, MD, MM, MBA, MHSA (Dr. David)

It is in your Moments of DECISION that your DESTINY is shaped.

—Tony Robbins

When we're candid and transparent about our journeys...

we are allowing people to be seen and heard and empowered

in ways they've never been.

—Gabrielle Union

David A. Wright, MD, MM, MBA, MHSA (Dr. David)

God never said that weapons wouldn't form against you.

He said that they wouldn't PROSPER.

—Isaiah 54:17

You are NOT Your PAST!

And, You are NOT What HAPPENED to You!

You are NO LONGER a VICTIM of Your Own STORY!

The Best Way to Look at AGING is to See it as an OPPORTUNITY to Leave What didn't work BEHIND and STEP BOLDLY into a Brand New FUTURE.

—Oprah Winfrey

In order to be HAPPY you must:

1. Let go of what's happened.

2. Be Grateful for what's left.

3. Look forward to what's next.

David A. Wright, MD, MM, MBA, MHSA (Dr. David)

Count Your BLESSINGS!

You NEVER know just HOW MUCH they may ADD up to!

Getting Older is INEVITABLE, Aging is OPTIONAL.

—Dr. Christiane Northrup

David A. Wright, MD, MM, MBA, MHSA (Dr. David)

Perhaps the most important thing that we give each other is our ATTENTION.

—Rachel Naomi Remen

Every time that you are tempted to react in the same old way,

Ask if you want to be

a Prisoner of the Past or

a Pioneer of the Future?

—Deepak Chopra, M.D.

David A. Wright, MD, MM, MBA, MHSA (Dr. David)

Until you make the Unconsious CONCIOUS,

It will direct your life and you will call it FATE.

—Carl Jung, Ph.D.

Life will bring pain all by itself.

Your responsibility is to create JOY.

—Milton Erickson, M.D.

David A. Wright, MD, MM, MBA, MHSA (Dr. David)

From error to error, one discovers the entire truth.

—Sigmund Freud, M.D.

Coaching transforms problems into challenges,

Challenges into opportunities, and

Opportunities into gifts.

—Milton Erickson, M.D.

The primary reason why most individuals in traditional talk therapies haven't achieved lasting change is because they've tried to achieve change by treating the symptoms on the surface, while allowing the deeper, real roots of their problems to fester, grow, flourish and thrive.

Problems are only TRULY solved at their source: THE ROOT CAUSE.

The ONLY Impossible Journey is the one that you Never BEGIN.

—Tony Robbins

David A. Wright, MD, MM, MBA, MHSA (Dr. David)

Live Your Life Like a DIAMOND!

Even a Stopped Clock keeps the right time, twice a day.

—Unknown

David A. Wright, MD, MM, MBA, MHSA (Dr. David)

Never argue with Stupid People.

They will drag you down to their level,

and then beat you with EXPERIENCE...

—Mark Twain

Turn your WOUNDS into WISDOM.

—Oprah Winfrey

The Biggest Adventure you can EVER take is to live the life of your DREAMS.

—Oprah Winfrey

Anything you can IMAGINE you can CREATE.

—Oprah Winfrey

David A. Wright, MD, MM, MBA, MHSA (Dr. David)

What I know is, if you do work that you love,

and the work fulfills you,

then the rest will come...

—Oprah Winfrey

You get in life what you have the COURAGE to ask for.

—Oprah Winfrey

When you undervalue what you do, the world will undervalue who you are.

—Oprah Winfrey

Listen to the Rhythm of your own calling, and follow that.

—Oprah Winfrey

CHAPTER 8

WRAPPING IT ALL UP

The idea for *Tomato Bisque for the Brain* came from watching episodes of *Super Soul Sunday* on the Oprah Winfrey Network (OWN). The purpose of *Tomato Bisque for the Brain* is to introduce you to methods, techniques, and resources that have helped me personally and professionally. I've used these methods, techniques, and resources to help my patients overcome addictions, defeat depression, annihilate anxiety, overcome symptoms of ADHD, move beyond grief, and vanquish symptoms of PTSD. I've also used these techniques and methods to help my clients who are seeking abundance, empowerment, courage, confidence, prosperity, and direction to successfully change careers, double their incomes, move past procrastination and stagnation, and re-create happiness and joy in their lives. *Tomato Bisque for the Brain* shows you how use every sensory modality that you have at your disposal to energize your thoughts, feelings, moods, actions, reactions, and belief systems so they become allies instead of enemies.

In addition to carrying two-thirds of a year's worth of motivational quotations and inspiration self-affirmations (in chapter 7), *Tomato Bisque for the Brain* also helps to enable you to move forward in positive, transformational ways by presenting you with techniques, methods, and strategies for controlling your mood, creating success, sideswiping negativity, escaping emotional and behavioral ruts, and resetting your mindset when needed. Once you have begun to let go of emotional, psychological, and mental baggage, discussed in chapter 1, you can begin surrounding yourself with like-minded individuals, coaches, mentors, and associates using the strategies in chapter 2. I like to call these "circles of trust and influence." After you have begun to create your new associations and relationships using the concepts presented within chapter 2, then you hit the reset switch by using the methods and techniques provided in chapter 3 to create a new direction and new pathways for an empowered journey. Once you have hit the reset switch by using the methods and techniques provided in chapter 3 to create a new direction and new pathways for an empowered journey, begin to use music and sound to create a new normal (as presented within chapter 4) for your mood and your ability to focus, concentrate, and achieve your goals. After you have begun to use music and sound to create a new normal for your mood and your ability to focus, concentrate, and achieve your goals (as presented within chapter 4), begin to use the power of your greatest somatic (i.e., bodily) sense and its associated mind and brain connections to start to really craft the life you desire (as presented in chapter 5). Once you have begun to use the power of your greatest somatic sense and its associated mind and brain connections to start to really craft the life you desire (as presented in chapter 5), move on to the next chapter and start using a method that will allow you to permanently defeat procrastination and to begin being more productive, efficient, and goal-directed than you've ever been before—using a simple system called the ROS (as presented within chapter 6). Finally, after you have started using the rank order system to permanently defeat procrastination and to begin being more productive, efficient, and goal-directed than you've ever been before (as presented in chapter 6), begin to use the positive motivational quotations and inspiring, mindset-based inspirational self-affirmations in chapter 7 to begin permanently changing your thoughts, feelings, and belief systems!

Together, these tools, methods, resources, strategies, and approaches will positively change the trajectory of your life—while simultaneously adding joy, happiness, and fulfillment to it! The keys to advancement are self-confidence, self-esteem, self-worth, goals, faith, planning, strategy, thoughts, feelings, beliefs, actions, and the courage to take carefully calculated risks. *Tomato Bisque for the Brain* will help you build a daily self-care regimen that works for you. It will help you to care for your mind, body, spirit, soul, and psyche in a way that empowers you daily while preventing frustration, stagnation, and exhaustion. And it draws upon cognitive, behavioral and alternative methodologies and techniques. Your history definitely helps to shape you. But the negative aspects of your history don't have to *define* you. You (and you alone) get to define, develop, and defend your desires and your destiny! You've started that journey to develop, define, and defend your desires and your destiny by using the techniques, methods, and resources described herein!

Along the way you might slip. You might even fall. But if you continue to employ the techniques and methods that you've learned in chapters 1 through 7, you will never, ever stay on the ground! You've become *tougher*! You've become *stronger*! You've become a *fighter*! That's what it takes to win the battle for your true *destiny*! It's all about those little steps that you take on a daily basis.

REFERENCES

Amory, Dean. *The Magic Power of Mental Images.* Belgium: Edgard
Adriaens.

Baker, Mitzi. "Music Moves Brain to Pay Attention, Stanford Study
Finds." Stanford Medicine. Accessed February 24, 2015.
https://plato.stanford.edu/entries/mental-imagery/.

"Beautiful Brains." *National Geographic*, November 22, 2011.

Bradt and Dileo. "Music for Stress and Anxiety Reduction in
Coronary Heart Disease Patients." PubMed.Gov, 2009.

"Brain Processing of Visual Information." MIT News, MIT Research,
MIT, December 19, 1996.

Burt, J. W. "Distant Thunder: Drumming with Vietnam Veterans."
Music Therapy Perspectives 13 (1995): 110–112; quoted in
Ronna Kaplan, "Music Therapy and the Military," *Huffington
Post*, March 4, 2013.

Conan, Neal. "Understanding the Mysterious Teenage Brain." NPR, September, 20, 2011.

Corso, Regina A. "The Glee Effect? More Americans Say Music Education Prepares People for Their Careers and Problem Solving Than in 2007." Harris Poll, July 24, 2014.

Dobbs, David. "A Troubling Adaptation: The Teenage Brain." *Wired*, September 15, 2011.

Ferguson and Sheldon. "Trying to Be Happier Really Can Work: Two Experimental Studies." *Journal of Positive Psychology* (2013).

Frazer, Valerie. "Concussion Recovery: Understanding Your Visual Symptoms," New Horizons Vision Therapy, March 13, 2019.

———. "Is it AD(H)D or Something Else?" New Horizons Vision Therapy, October 30, 2019.

———. "Surprising Reasons Many Children Avoid Reading." New Horizons Vision Therapy, January 15, 2019.

Grady, Denise. "The Vision Thing: Mainly in the Brain." *Discover*, June 1, 1993.

Hagen, Susan. "The Mind's Eye: How Do We Transform an Ever-Changing Jumble of Visual Stimuli into the Rich and Coherent Three-Dimensional Perception We Know as Sight?" *Rochester Review* 74, no. 4 (March–April 2012).

"Is It True or False that Vision Rules the Brain?" Image Think, November 20, 2012.

King, Paul. "How Much of the Brain Is Involved with Vision? What about Hearing, Touch, Etc.?" Quora, September 28, 2013.

Kohen, D. P., K. N. Olness, S. O. Colwell, and A. Heimel. "The Use of Relaxation-Mental Imagery (Self-Hypnosis) in the Management of 505 Pediatric Behavioral Encounters." *Journal of Developmental and Behavioral Pediatrics* 5, no. 1 (February 1984): 21–25.

Kraus, N., and B. Chandrasekaran. "Music Training for the Development of Auditory Skills." *Neuroscience* (November 2010): 599–605.

Kraus, Nina, and Dana L. Strait. "Emergence of Biological Markers of Musicianship with School-Based Music Instruction." *Annals of the New York Academy of Sciences* (2015).

Kriegeskorte, Nikolaus. "Deep Neural Networks: A New Framework for Modeling Biological Vision and Brain Information Processing." *Annual Review of Vision Science* 1 (November 2015): 417–46. https://doi.org/10.1146/annurev-vision-082114-035447.

Logeswaran et al. "Cross-Modal Transfer of Emotion by Music." *Neuroscience Letters* (2009).

"Mental Imagery." *Stanford Encyclopedia of Philosophy*, Spring 2007. First published November 18, 1997; revised August 4, 2005.

Pallesen et al. "Cognitive Control in Auditory Working Memory Is Enhanced in Musicians." *PLOS One*, June 15, 2010.

Politzer, Thomas. "Vision Is Our Dominant Sense," BrainLine, November 6, 2008.

Preidt, Robert. "Music Therapy Might Help People with Epilepsy," HealthDay, August 10, 2015.

Rogers, Kara. "Mental Imagery: The Power of the Mind's Eye." *Encyclopedia Britannica* blog, September 2008.

Romane, Vance. "Hypnotic Pain Control, and the Power of Affirmations versus Mental Imagery," March 10, 2016. VanceRomane.com.

Rose, Nikolas. "Reading the Human Brain: How the Mind Became Legible." *Body & Society* 22, no 2: 140–77.

Skoe, E., and N. Kraus. 2012. "A Little Goes a Long Way: How the Adult Brain Is Shaped by Musical Training in Childhood." *Journal of Neuroscience* (2012): 32, 34. https://doi.org/10.1523/JNEUROSCI.1949-12.2012.

Stein, Traci. "7 Tips for Creating Positive Mental Imagery: How You Can Harness Your Imagination to Improve Your Body, Mind, and Life." *Psychology Today*, June 18, 2013.

"Vision: Processing Information," BrainFacts, April 1, 2012.

INDEX OF RESEARCH STUDIES, CASE REPORTS, CLINICAL TRIALS, ARTICLES, AUTHORS AND EXPERTS

INDEX

Tomato Bisque for the Brain is a book of wisdom, abundance, empowerment, prosperity and success.

- It is the best way to increase your self-improvement, self-development, self-motivation, self-reflection, self-actualization, self-determination, self-transformation and self-enhancement on a daily basis!

- In addition to carrying 2/3rds of a year's worth of motivational quotations and inspirational self-affirmations (in Chapter 7), this book also helps to enable you to move forward in positive, transformational ways by presenting you with techniques, methods and strategies for helping you control your mood, create success, sideswipe negativity, escape emotional and behavioral ruts, and reset your mindset when needed.

- Chapter One covers Emotion Hoarding
- Chapter Two covers how to create circles of trust, empowerment and abundance in your life
- Chapter Three shows you how to create and press the "RESET" Switch in life
- Chapter Four covers the power of sound and music to enhance life
- Chapter Five covers the topic of mental imagery to create the future that you desire
- Chapter Six contains a sure psychological strategy for prioritizing tasks and simplifying the process of decision-making
- Chapter Seven provides you with two thirds (2/3) of a year of motivational quotes, inspirational phrases and daily positive self-affirmations

Together, the chapters of this book will empower you with success-driving techniques while also providing you with the basic concepts, underpinnings and foundation for the formation of the habits upon which healthy mindsets and success are built.

—David A. Wright, MD, MM, MBA, MHSA

"*Tomato Bisque for the Brain* is inspiring. It taps into the very essence of self-esteem building and affirmation. Dr. Wright manages to boost the spirits of readers by employing short, straight-to-the-point quotes that are enabling, timely, emotionally tranquilizing, and useful for readers. These quotes are spiritually rich in nature and can, like a hot bowl of tomato bisque soup, indeed lift your spirits, allay your cravings, and comfort you."

—Dr. Bettye Dunn-Wright
University of Arkansas at Pine Bluff
Associate Professor, School of Education, Curriculum and Instruction
Past School District Superintendent & Elementary School Principal

"*Tomato Bisque for the Brain* is an outstanding addition to the motivational self-help field as we have been awaiting a compendium of practical self-help quotes and positive affirmations. Individuals struggling with stress, anxiety, life direction, or challenges and obstacles will find this immensely valuable. I have known Dr. Wright for over ten years. He is an intelligent, observant, levelheaded, practical, and innovative thinker in the mental health field. This should be required reading for all individuals who struggle with purpose and direction!"

—Todd M. Antin, MD
Board certified in adult, addiction, forensic, and geriatric psychiatry
CEO and Medical Director of PACT Atlanta LLC
Psychiatry Department Medical Director for Emory DeKalb Medical Center

U.S. $XX.XX
ISBN 978-1-6632-0989-4
90000

iUniverse®

Printed in the United States
by Baker & Taylor Publisher Services